A WALK ALONG THE ERIE'S NEWBURGH BRANCH

ISBN # 978-0-615-34582-6

A WALK ALONG THE ERIE'S NEWBURGH BRANCH
By Robert McCue

(Title page) Departing Newburgh, 1925   The Erie's station is visible to the right of the engine. The New York Central's West Shore station is visible to the left.
C. Davis photo, Russell Hallock collection

(Next page) The Erie's Newburgh station
The walkway being built across the West Shore
   Tracks was added when the West Shore's
      (New York Central) was built in 1914.
   The engine in the lower picture is Baldwin- built
909 Built 7/1901, scrapped 7/1927
Picture taken, 1925   J.H. Dean photo   *Russell Hallock*

Table of contents

Preface/many thanks to...   vi

Foreword: A few thoughts on a roadbed... xii

Introduction-In 1976...   Page 1

Dedication...   Page 11

Growing up on the branch/Postscript:
    Edward J. McLaughlin...   Page 19

What's old is new, The Graham line...   Page 35

New Windsor to Washingtonville...   Page 43

Washingtonville to Greycourt
and beyond...   Page 83

The New York, Ontario and
Western Railroad, and the
Erie's "shortcut"...   Page 125

Harriman monument:
"What Hath God Wrought"
    ..Page 143-144

A view from the
High View tunnel:
   Ron Britzke...   Page 161

Twilight on the Newburgh branches...   Page 171

Photo Gallery: Under the brow of Schunemunk...Page 177

Dennis Carpenter

Preface

"Don't take it to the grave"

The generations that came before us compiled, in both words and photographs, a record of their life and times that is second to none. Now the time has come when it is our responsibility to preserve for future generations our proud history. In that spirit *A walk along the Erie's Newburgh branch* marks the closing of a chapter in our country's history that we shall not see the likes of again.

Situated on the west shore of the Hudson River, the city of Newburgh was once linked by the Erie Railroad to seven other towns and the Erie's own mainline. There are only five miles, from Newburgh to Vails Gate, that survive of this once bustling rail line today. The book you are about to read looks at the fourteen miles of this railroad line that was abandoned in 1984.

My first walk on the Erie roadbed all those years ago was only the first piece in a giant puzzle. On the following pages is my many thanks to the people whose generosity and support helped put the pieces together.

Every writer starts out at day one thinking they have a firm knowledge of their subject. It's every day that comes after that teaches you different. I can say with pride and affection that every revision I have done or will do as new pieces of the puzzle come in remind me that even after more than twenty years I am still an apprentice at this craft.

Photo credits: Walter Kierzkowski, Ronald Vassallo, Russell Hallock, Douglas Barberio and Blake Tatar, of the New York, Ontario and Western Railway Historical Society.

If I could not fit every map and photo that was offered in, the great support given to this project still has to be given proper thank you all the same.

Further photo credits go to: the Chester Historical Society, the Woodbury Historical society and Glenn Marshall, the town of New Windsor Historian

Dennis Carpenter, whose firsthand memories come from having family who worked on the branch

All maps marked United States Geological Survey (USGS) are from the New Hampshire Diamond Library map site.

Additional maps: Google earth

Any pictures without credit are from the
Author's collection

To Janet Dempsey, Cornwall Historian and the staff at the old Cornwall-on-Hudson Library where this all began on those after school afternoons long ago.

A thank you also, to Irene Sheldon. Almost twenty summers have flown by since Irene turned my firsthand written pages into the first typed *COUNTRY COUSINS* manuscript.

The old Cornwall on Hudson Library

Dennis Carpenter

NEW YORK AND ERIE RAILROAD TIME TABLE.

No. 9.   NEWBURGH BRANCH.   **No. 9.**

For the Government and Information of Employes only, and is not intended for the information of the Public; the Company reserve the right to vary therefrom as circumstances may require.

TAKES EFFECT MONDAY, MAY 19, 1856.

EASTWARD TRAINS.					WESTWARD TRAINS.			
2d CLASS.	FIRST CLASS.			NAMES OF STATIONS.	FIRST CLASS.			2d CLASS.
FREIGHT.	No. 4.		No. 2.		No. 1.		No. 3.	FREIGHT.
2.30PM	8.25PM	----	10 35AM	Ar. Newburgh, Dep.	7.00AM	----	5.10PM	12.00 M
1.56 "	8 08 "	----	10 17 "	Dep. Vail's Gate. -	7.15 "	----	5.25 "	12.30PM
1.32 "	7 57 "	----	10.06 "	- Salisbury. -	7.27 "	----	5.38 "	12. 52 "
1.18 "	7.49 "	----	9.58 "	- Washingtonville, -	7.33 "	----	5.45 "	**1.18** "
12 31 "	7.35 "	----	9.41 "	- Craigsville, -	7.47 "	----	6.00 "	1.46 "
----	----	----	----	- East Junction, -	----	----	----	----
12 15PM	*7.28 "	----	*9.57 "	- West Junction, -	*7.53 "	----	*6 07 "	2.00 "
----	7.25 "	----	9 35 "	- Chester. -	8.00 "	----	6 15 "	----
----	7.12 "	----	9.18 "	- Goshen, -	8.12 "	----	6.24 "	----
----	7.03 "	----	9.08 "	- Hampton, -	8.22 "	----	6.32 "	----
----	6.55PM	----	9.00AM	Dep. Middletown. Ar.	8.30AM	----	6.40PM	----
----	----	----	----	----	----	----	----	----

LOOK OUT FOR SIGNALS ON TRACK!

Rule 5.—Supplementary Instructions, May 15th, 1854.—"A Red Flag by day, and a Lantern by night, when swung upon the Track; a Torpedo exploded thereon; the absence of Lights at Switches and Crossings where usually shown; and all Signals violently given, are Signals of Danger. On perceiving either, the Engineer must bring the Train to a DEAD STOP; nor shall he receive any information from any Flagman or other person, until the Train is brought to a STAND."

☞ An Extra Train following a regular Train will approach all Stations and Wooding Places with great care, expecting to find the preceding Train taking Wood or Water at such Station, whether it may be a stopping place, as per Time Table, for that Train or not, and the responsibility of a collision will rest upon the Conductor and Engineer of the Extra Train; but the Conductor of the leading Train will not deviate from rules 7 and 8, Supplementary Instructions, May, 15, 1854, nor shall he inform the Conductor or Engineer of the following Train as to what place he intends to take Wood and Water.

PETER WARD, Sup't, N. B. R. R., Newburgh.   **D. C. McCALLUM, Gen'l Sup't.**

West Newburgh engine house   *Russell Hallock collection*

> *"When we build, let us think we build forever. Let it not be for the present delight nor for the present use alone. Let it be such work as our descendents will thank us for, and let us think, as we lay stone on stone, that a time will come when these stones will be held sacred because our hands will have touched them, and that men will say, as they look upon the labor and wrought substance of them, "See! This our father did for us"*
> John Ruskin

Foreword

Walk down a mountain railroad right of way, with its path winding its way through rock cuts and over high trestles, and it's easy to imagine giant steam engines battling to get the cargo in their charge over the next summit. All amid sounds akin to the hammers of hell as these massive engines spew out great masses of steam, smoke and sand in their struggle. On the other side of the coin a walk down a right of way meandering through rolling countryside can conjure up images of Gingerbread style stations and mixed trains of freight, mail and milk cars. Mixed trains pulled by smaller, veteran steam engines that were once the star performers of mainline service.

Mountain or countryside, you could walk down the same right of way for twenty years and no two trips are ever going to be alike, whether it be for reasons of nature or otherwise. Fall covers as many relics of the past as it reveals.

Deep snow reminds us of the railroad's battle against the elements. Spring lines the side of the roadbed with skunk cabbage and the trout lilies. Summer brings out the hikers, the dog walkers and the rollerbladers to the roadbeds that have been taken under the wing of the rails to trails movement. But those who have hiked the same trails for many years realize that as they change over time so does the right of way they thought they knew like their second skin. Storms reveal elements that may have been covered for years. And familiar buildings that had stood against the elements for a hundred years finally have to give way.

Walk a right of way for the first time and it will instantly give away as many secrets as it hides. Overgrown sections of track left intact out in the middle of nowhere. Mile markers and whistle posts that in their simple former purpose speak volumes of distance from railroad points long vanished.

Finding the occasional boxcar shell that spent its last days in railroad service as a section house only to be left behind, ignored by the scrapper's torch when the rails were pulled, speaks volumes of generations that came before.

In life the railroad's battle against the elements was relentless. In death the roadbeds left behind are still in a constant battle against the elements and progress.

Some will be left intact as trails for all time while others will succumb to the needs of the next generation to come along. That the world must move on is a given, to move on without respecting what came before is a tragedy. There is no new highway, no housing project, or new mega mall that is built today on virgin land. Whether it was railroad bed or farmer's field, someone in the past put their sweat, blood and maybe even their life into that land to have something to pass onto the next generation.

If you put a handful of the past in your hand, either farmer's sod or brick from an abandoned building, someone from the past is holding it with you.

Robert McCue

The Poughkeepsie bridge **(Above)** has been reopened as a public walkway.

Dennis Carpenter

Climbing the grade away from Newburgh waterfront

The area around Newburgh had a maze of sidings and industrial spurs which served everything from coal yards to lumber yards to factories. All of which will be covered in depth in a future book.

Introduction: Conrail arrives in 1976

1976 was the year of America's two hundredth Birthday. The history of America's Railroads had encompassed three-quarters of two hundred years. One of these railroads was to become a legend in her time-the Erie Railroad. Planning and construction of the Erie had progressed through the 1830's and 1840's. The official opening ceremonies came on May 14th, 1851. The railroad that was to become famous for her engineering feats started out in life as America's longest railroad-446 miles.

Only a hundred years would separate the beginning of the Erie's best years from the beginning of the worst. In the 1950's the Erie Railroad and the it's long standing rival-the Delaware, Lackawanna and Western Railroad (DL&W)- would be just two of the many railroads doomed by the coming of America's new interstate highway system. The Erie and the DL&W would merge in 1959-1960.

Two rivals combining their resources at the beginning of what was to prove to be the darkest of days for the American Railroad business.

In 1960 the Erie-Lackawanna was one of four railroads coming into the massive Maybrook freight yard in Orange County, N.Y. The other three were the Lehigh and Hudson Railroad, the Lehigh and New England Railroad and the New Haven Railroad. Maybrook yard's lifeblood was freight being shipped to and from the New England states. All via the New Haven Railroad and its route that took it over the mile long Railroad Bridge at Poughkeepsie. A fifth railroad-the New York, Ontario and Western-came into Maybrook until it's closing in March of 1957. The Lehigh and New England would join the O&W in the railroad hereafter in October of 1961.

By the start of the 1970's the New Haven Railroad had become part of newly formed Penn Central Railroad.

The Penn Central was born out of the merger of two dying railroad giants-the New York Central and the Pennsylvania. The government's approval of the Penn Central merger hinged on the addition of the New Haven, who was in midst of its own dire straits.

On May 8th, 1974, a fire on the Poughkeepsie Railroad Bridge would put an end for all time to rail service on the bridge. Closing the bridge would seal the fate of Maybrook's rail yard. And with Maybrook went Orange County's days as a major rail hub.

On April 1st 1976, the Erie-Lackawanna, the Lehigh and Hudson River and the Penn Central were three of the six bankrupt railroads merged by the federal government into Conrail-the Consolidated Rail Corporation. Conrail would now begin in the name of economics the dismantling of the railroad network that had once been a symbol of America's industrial might.

One of the many rail lines to fall victim to the scrapper's torch was the Erie's Newburgh branch.

Leaving the Erie mainline at Greycourt, the branch had railroad stations at Craigville, Blooming Grove, Washingtonville and Salisbury Mills.

The towns of Vails Gate and New Windsor were the last two stations on the branch before coming into Newburgh. Here the Erie joined the West Shore Railroad. (Text continues on page 8)

(Last page) Greycourt, circa early 1970's
Russell Hallock
The line to Newburgh curves of to the left
(arrow) By the time this picture was taken
Greycourt station is gone (concrete patch
to the left of L&HR) and weeds are
starting to overtake the Erie-Lackawanna
mainline. The merger of the
Lehigh and Hudson River Railroad and
the Erie Lackawanna into Conrail is just over
the horizon.

(Below) Motorcar trip, Vails Gate May 1983
Come fall of 1983 Conrail would begin removing
the rails from the switch in the background to
Greycourt. The *coup de grace* would come a few
years later with the filling in of the
Thruway bridge just a half mile ahead of
where this picture was taken. Breaking the
connection between Newburgh and Greycourt for
all time.

Compare the picture below with the Vails Gate
photo on page 46.

Jim Parella photo, Russell Hallock collection

Salisbury Mills **(Top)** 1971 Dennis Carpenter

(Bottom) July, 1983
Jim Parella photo, Russell Hallock collection

(Above) "Snow covered and long out of use" was the caption for this picture that was used in a *Newburgh Evening News* newspaper article. The article was written in 1984 about a local group that was attempting to save the historic rail line through Washingtonville from the scrap train and turn it into a line for local freight and tourist trains. The scrap train was already pulling the rails just downtrack.

Original Photo, inset, Ward Poche

In 1981 the Erie's Newburgh branch was out of use, but still intact. The station at Washingtonville was standing as it had for a century, right down to the signboard on the depot. Only the heavy brush growing over the rusted rails told of the one missing key element. I was sixteen and on my bike when I first came across this corner of the world that seemed frozen in time. In the days before the housing boom, the eight mile bike ride out to Washingtonville was truly a ride in the country.

In the years that followed I would be back time and time again as bike rides turned into day long hikes out on the roadbed. Removal of the tracks starting in late 1983 had cleared the roadbed of brush for the first time in many years.

Rt. 208 crossing and milepost G7 (Greycourt) 7

It takes about two and half hours to make the eight mile walk from Cornwall to Washingtonville. And that now familiar depot roofline sticking out up ahead from behind the trees was to become like a greeting from an old friend.

Standing just yards from the old roadbed today, I look at the traffic that clogs the intersection of Rt.94 and Rt. 208 and wonder about what might have been. With every empty railroad bed and every empty lonesome depot is a lesson to be learned.

E.J. McLaughlin photo, Russell Hallock collection

(Top) 1981 **(Bottom)** 1985

Dedication

All vivid firsthand memories, as well as the pen and ink drawings of the station and bridges found in Country Cousins, come from Washingtonville Historian, Edward J. McLaughlin. From his memories also comes the story of the blizzard of '47 that put life back into an empty roadbed and remind me why I wanted to write this book. I could never have thanked him enough. In the years since the first book came out in print, Edward McLaughlin has left us for that better place. A lover of history and a friend to all, he is sorely missed. This second edition is dedicated to him. But I also have to add a dedication with two stories you will read here (One coming up next, one on page 161) to the dedicated workers on all railroads who keep the trains running through the best and the worst.

2007

E.J. McLaughlin

Intro to Bradley's cut

The first lesson in writing is the book is about the writing, not about the writer. I have always given the credit to Mr. McLaughlin's story of the blizzard of 1947 for reminding me what I was writing Country Cousins for in the first place. Anyone who says that writing a book, especially their first one, does not inflate the ego is full of...themselves.

When I started work on this book (First titled Country Cousins II, Coming home) *A walk along the Erie's Newburgh branch* was all on computer: scan, download, and paste. The memories of day long walks on the roadbeds, the thrill of discovering that forgotten mile marker or the unexpected bridge, was becoming without me even realizing it a case of *Been there, done that.* Then amid a story Walter Kierzkowski mailed me about the Moodna Viaduct was the story of Bradley's cut on the Graham line that brought back the human element like the blizzard of '47 had done some twenty years before.

The kind of story that sticks in your head that has to be told.

There are few things to stir the spirit like the sight of a massive steam engine coming around the bend in a great mass of steam, smoke and flying connecting rods. And astride all this is the waving hand of the Engineer who holds the lives of his train and its crew in his hands. To the passerby it is almost impossible to realize how easily the unexpected can turn this hundreds of tons of smoking mechanical grace into the worst imaginable kind of carnage. But for the railroad crews it rides on their mind on every turn in the track. It is to these men that this book is further dedicated: To anyone lost, in spirit or body, to the rhythm of the rails and the sound of the whistle in the night. Their ghosts are on every curve.

Bradley's cut

Manville Wakefield-circa late 1940's

Along the cutoff there are many large cuts, notably the one known as the Four Story Cut, just east of Middletown, whose name is most descriptive as it is a cut of extreme depth. West of Howells station is Bradley's cut, noted not so much for its large proportions, but for the way in which it got its name. It is named after Engineer J.J. Bradley, who along with his fireman and brakeman lost his life early on the morning of August 5, 1910, in the first wreck on the freight line. Engineer L.W. Hinkley, who still highballs fast freights out of Port Jervis, relates how his westbound freight No. 77 was the last train passing through the cut before the ill-fated eastbound 78.

Hinkley at the time was a fireman while Sam Clark was holding down the right hand side. At Tower FX, where the freight line joins the main line at the top of Port Jervis Hill, Hinkley waved to his friend Bradley for the last time as both trains passed in the night. In the cab of engine 2527 with Bradley was Fireman H.E. Taylor and Brakeman George Carpenter. A severe electrical storm was raging that night high up in the Shawangunks as No. 78 highballed through the Otisville tunnel and on towards the cut, then called Crystal Run, just west of Howells. All boards were green as 78 pounded around the curve at 1:50 a.m. to enter the cut. Across the tracks a huge 400 –ton shale boulder, 6 feet thick and ten-feet across, had slid from the top of the 75 foot cut to the track below some time after the passage of No. 77. It rested across the tracks in such a manner that the circuits were not broken, therefore the blocks remained green, giving No.78 a clear track.

After striking the rock the engine went 250 feet before tipping over on the opposing main, the cab completely demolished. Only the boiler, drivers, and frame were left intact. Fireman Taylor's watch stopped at 1:53 a.m., the exact time of the wreck. The first wrecking crew arrived from Port Jervis about 3a.m. and at 6:30 a.m. another wrecker came from Jersey City. Just after daybreak two dismembered bodies were scooped out of the tangled wreckage of the K-1 locomotive, and a third body was found under the splintered wreckage of the car behind the tender. Beyond this pile of debris lay 30 wrecked and derailed freight cars, most carrying fresh fruit and produce.

What caused the rock to slide?
That's the mystery of Bradley's cut.

Russell Hallock

The Newburgh branch
Myself standing on the old iron bridge below Washingtonville

Old iron bridge   *E.J. McLaughlin*

Growing up on the branch By Edward J. McLaughlin

Growing up in Washingtonville, I would awaken in the morning to the whistle of the west-bound local passenger and mail train on the Erie's Newburgh branch. My home was within sight of the rails and the Depot across Moodna Creek. It was my signal to start for school.

The way freight coming out from Newburgh would pause at the big old wrought iron truss bridge where the "the branch" crossed. The Head Brakeman would throw the switch for the passing track just west of the bridge and the freight of sometimes twenty-five assorted cars would pull into the switch.

There would be an hour or more of the constant shuffling of cars in and out of Seacord and Cooper Brother's lumber, coal and feed mill house tracks. And then more train movements were to be made at Frank Brown's coal and feed store and perhaps a car of glass milk bottles or coal for the Borden's Creamery.

The two crossings in the village would add to my delight with numerous whistles and bell ringing. Of course Mr. Robert Barret would come out of his tiny watchman's shanty at the South Street crossing (Route 208) and stand in the roadway holding a short pole with a round white sign lettered "STOP".

An eastbound passenger train would hurry through the yard and stop at the depot while the way-freight waited patiently on the siding. These diminutive passenger trains were usually made up of a combination baggage, mail, express and smoker followed by another coach. Motive power was provided by the H20 class consolidations (2-8-0 wheel Arrangement) numbered in the 1500-2000 series. The same type of locomotive was also used on the freight trains.

When switching was completed, and the Conductor received his orders from the Dispatcher, the way-freight would whistle off and pull out of the siding to the main track at the big girder bridge over the Moodna just east of the Borden plant. The rear brakeman would swing aboard the caboose after locking the switch and the sturdy consolidation would storm towards Greycourt trying to the consist moving as it climbed the climbed the grade toward Blooming Grove. I would strain my ears listening for the two longs and two shorts of the whistle at the Blooming Grove crossing.

The afternoon would see two more passenger runs to the east and west. The way-freight, now east-bound, would deposit more loads in the yard.

Sometimes there would be a tank car of wine from Brotherhood's Kingsburg, California winery to be blended at America's oldest winery located on North Street. Occasionally, a stock car would bring a new herd of heifers to the stock pen at the east end of the freight house which had its own switch. The afternoon westbound passenger would pick up three or four refrigerated cars of bottled milk and cream from the Borden's switch and hustle them off to the mainline at Greycourt to connect with a milk train eastbound to Jersey City.

Sunday afternoon was a real treat for me, as a young boy when my Dad would take me on a hike through the woods to the old truss bridge. We would cross it on the wooden catwalk built to allow the brakemen to walk past the standing train as it waited for the passing switch to be thrown.

Dad would point out the plaque on the bridge showing its construction date 1871. Two barrels were buried in the cinder right-of-way at each end of the bridge filled with water to be used as emergency fire extinguishers.

One year, Theo Clark of Salisbury Mills-the maintenance of way Foreman, and his crew erected the coveted "Prize section" sign near the Washingtonville freight house. This meant the track and right-of-way was in top condition.

Some afternoons, after school, I would walk down Depot Street to the station and visit with the agent Edward Parks. He would be busy writing up freight bills, telephoning recipients of express and freight shipments. His duties included stoking the big pot-bellied stove in the twenty by twenty foot waiting room and another stove in the agent's office plus dozens of other tasks.

Text continues on page 27

(Last page, top) *Russell Hallock*
(Last page, bottom) Station interior, 1990
(Above and right) Interior trimwork
(Below) Newburgh's West Shore station

Mr. Parks would frequently call the train Dispatcher in Jersey City on the telephone to "OS" the passenger trains or to receive train orders which would come over the telegraph line. He would walk through the yard each day and report the number of each standing freight car on the various switches.

Whenever a train was due he would roll out the heavy hand cart to be placed beside the baggage car door when the train stopped. Then there was also unloading of baggage, mail bags and express items that had to be signed upon receipt. Heavy pieces that a small man like Mr. Parks seemed to handle with ease. Of course, there were tickets to be sold, questions to be answered for waiting railroad passengers as to connections at either end of the branch.

The freight house inventory had to be taken daily and its doors unlocked for customers who came to pick up their freight.

Even with all these unending chores, Mr. Parks could find time to chat with me and allow me to listen on the dispatcher's open telephone line as various agents on the New York division of the Erie Railroad reported trains passing their stations. The station agent was responsible for sending and receiving telegrams of Western Union telegraph Company.

Friday afternoons would find me pushing an old Caldwell fourteen-inch mower across James Burnett's lawn. I would finish this on Saturday morning and receive fifty cents. The person who rides his power mower on this lawn today receives fifty dollars. Hurrying with a buddy to the depot we would board the 11:30AM train for Newburgh. The great depression was upon us and the steam powered trains were being handled by a Brill motor car operated by an engineer and conductor.

The fare was twenty-five cents for a round trip which gave me fifteen cents for a matinee movie at the Cameo or Academy Theater. A lone dime bought one of those famous Texas Weiners.

I would hurry down Broadway, down the steps of the small park at the end of South Water Street and through the West Shore station to the Erie depot on the lower level on Front Street. The late afternoon Brill Motor car, which some called the "hinkey-dink" or the "Toonerville," would bring me home to Washingtonville about 6PM.

Hudson Transit Bus Company began motor coach operations in competition with the Erie's many branches in Orange County and by 1935 the much loved passenger trains ceased to run. In the final year steam locomotives were used again as the old Brill cars were wearing out. The mainline train No. 54, the "Tuxedo" east-bound and No.57 westbound began at Newburgh running to Greycourt and thence east to Jersey City.

These trains were powered by Class E Atlantics (4-4-2) in the 500 numbered series. Some trips were made by the 900 numbered Class G ten Wheelers. (4-6-0) Freight service continued on the branch until 1979, diesel powered through the Erie-Lackawanna merger and into the Conrail era, when the branch was terminated from Vail's Gate Junction to Greycourt. A few years later a demolition crew tore up the rails and stockpiled the usable ties to be sold.

My love of the railroad continued through forty years of commuting from Washingtonville to New York City. For many years, the trip was made with steam power in Stillwell coaches with K-1 Pacifics (4-6-2) of the 2500 series. Many trips were made with the famous Alco 50,000 locomotive number 2509. Later the K-4 Pacifics in the 2700 series powered the Jersey City to Port Jervis commuter trains followed by the K5A heavy Pacifics in the 2900 series.

The diesel era began with the ALCO PA's and later the E3 and E8's powered the long commuter runs into the Conrail era.

With the takeover by Metro-North Commuter Railroad contracting with Jersey Transit, new locomotives and sleek stainless steel air conditioned coaches using a push-pull arrangement were employed.

When the Erie's low grade Graham line used for heavy freights was refurbished and passenger moved from the old mainline to the Graham line, a new Salisbury Mills/Cornwall Station was built at the north end of the famous Moodna Viaduct. Ample parking and a faster trip to the Hoboken Terminal is a commuter's delight.

Plaque on the new commuter station, Salisbury Mills *1990*

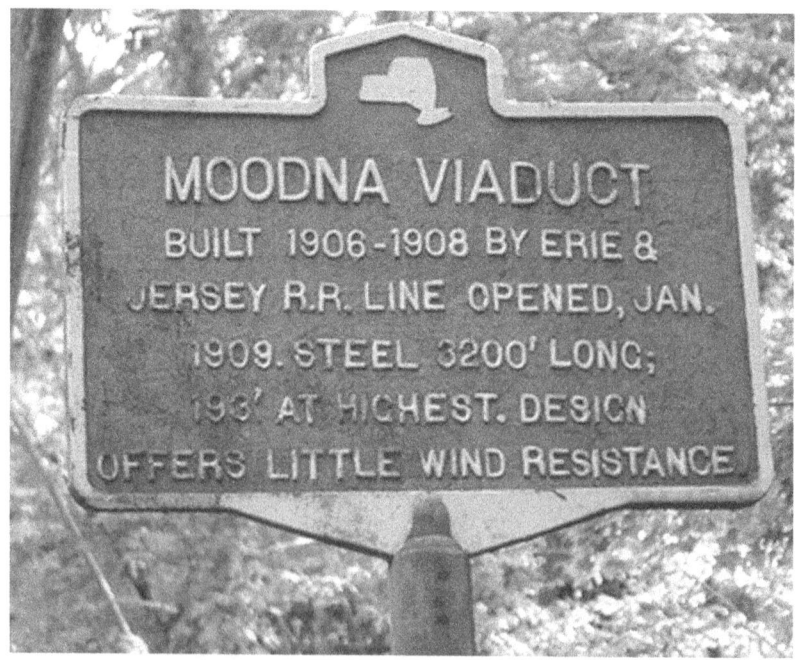

A MAMMOTH UNDERTAKING

The Erie's Great New Railroad Enterprise FOR A LOWER GRADE

In regard to the new freight line about to be constructed by the Erie it may be said that work will begin in a fortnight, at least in two of the five sections into which the work has been divided. Contractors are now busy getting machinery, derricks, steam shovels, and rails on the ground, and erecting shanties for the use of the workers.

The line will cost $1,250.000 and is the most important public railroad or other work undertaken in a given space in Orange County. It will be a double tracked road extending from Newburgh Junction, on the main line of the Erie, through Central Valley via Highland Mills, Woodbury, Schunemunk Mountain, Houghton farm, Mountainville, across Moodna Creek to Campbell Hall, where it will join the main line again.

> This is a copy that was made from part of a much longer newspaper article that appeared in the Orange County Times-Press on Tuesday, April 3, 1906.

(Last page and below) Two vivid reminders of the power of nature: The chalk mark that was made on this abutment after the floods of April of 2007 is at head height. And two weeks after the original article on the last page appeared, the news of any and all great enterprises like the coming of the Erie's new freight line would be knocked off the front page by the great San Francisco earthquake.

Postscript
E.J. McLaughlin

December 26, 1947, an unusual snowstorm struck the east coast. By early afternoon the storm had reached blizzard strength. I was working at an advertising agency in midtown Manhattan when it became imperative that if I was able to return home, I should leave as soon as possible. Upon reaching Jersey City's Erie Terminal via the old Hudson and Manhattan Railroad (Hudson Tubes) I found a jam of commuters trying to reach their train or any train running on the Erie. Slowly the Erie men were able to dispatch a train from one track (out of twelve) in the terminal to various branches and the main lines. Finally boarding a train at 7 PM bound for Port Jervis, it was packed with standees and making every station stop. I arrived in Monroe about 9:30 PM.

Digging my car out of the drifting snow, I was able to follow a snowplow north on Route 208 to Washingtonville. The snow was about thirty inches deep on the level by that hour.

To its credit, the Erie Railroad and its dedicated railroaders were able to get all their passengers home that night. The Delaware, Lackawanna and Western, Central Railroad of New Jersey, Long Island, New York New Haven and Hartford, Pennsylvania and New York Central Railroads, all closed down completely stranding passengers at terminals and even aboard trains stuck in snow drifts out on the line.

Erie men struggled to keep switch points from freezing in the teeth of a howling blizzard, engineers and firemen urged on their old dependable steamers, conductors and brakemen helped their passengers safely off at all the many stations and the Erie Railroad stood proud that terrible night.

Edward J. McLaughlin, Railroad Historian

What's old is new: The Graham line
Robert McCue

If you make the daily commute today from anywhere in Orange County, N.Y. to New York City, what would your reaction be to the news that the powers to be running the commuter service were planning to build a new commuter line. Here's the plan, 42 miles of rail line laid out in such a way that it will service the heart of the county's booming Real Estate market: the ever growing towns and outlying areas of Harriman and Chester, Washingtonville and Blooming Grove, Campbell Hall and Montgomery, Middletown and Wallkill, and Otisville. The line will also take heavy freight train traffic out of the center of some of our most bustling neighborhoods along the old railroad line. Worried about vehicle traffic-the entire line will be above grade, not a road crossing on the entire railroad line! Groundbreaking will begin in 1906.

Yes-1906! The commuter line service we take for granted today was built back when the area known today for its urban sprawl was open farmland and Henry Ford had yet to come out with his Model T! A railroad company called the Erie would build this new line with as level a grade as possible to accommodate the freight trains and steam engines that were becoming longer and heavier. The line would open in 1909, less than three years. In modern times, what public mass transit plan even gets past the planning stage in three years?

Let's go back to the first decade of the twentieth century. Theodore Roosevelt was in the white house. The America he presided over was coming of age as a global power, the American Wild West having been closed only a quarter of a century before. We had in our midst aging veterans who had once been young men who fought in the battle of Bull Run and Gettysburg. No one could know that the next war, more horrible than possible to imagine at the time, was a decade away.

Here on the dawn of the auto and air age was the golden era of America's railroads. In New York City, work was beginning, just blocks away from each other, for two of the grandest railroad stations the world would ever see. Guiding the fortunes of this railroad empire were men with names such as the likes of Vanderbilt and Harriman that crisscrossed America's history like the web of railroads they built. Often using less than legal business maneuvering that would gain for them the infamous nickname "The Robber Barons".

E.H Harriman would be part of the brain trust that would bring noted engineer James Graham to build the Erie's new freight line, named the Guymard Cutoff for the town at its most northern junction with the mainline. Graham already had to show among his long list of accomplishments realigning the Union Pacific's Great Salt Lake route, and Washington D.C.'s magnificent new Union station. He was also involved at the same time with electrifying the Erie's line through Rochester.

This was only part of an extensive list of ongoing projects the fifty year old Graham was involved in as the new century dawned.* Maybe in the end however, the workload was a case of "too many irons in the fire" as Graham died suddenly in February of 1909.

The Moodna Viaduct had opened in January of 1909, completing the Erie's new cutoff that would be renamed in Graham's honor. Some eighty years later, the powers that be had enough funding to upgrade either the Erie mainline or the Graham line, but not both, for both freight and commuter service. Embracing the idea of up to date rail service without the bottleneck of mile long freights crossing through the center of town at grade would write a new chapter in the Erie story. It also doomed the venerable Erie mainline to the scrapper. *

*Bibliography: "Erie Memories" by Ed Crist
And further thanks to Walter Kierzkowski

(Top and below) Replacement work on the Viaduct's concrete piers (fall, 2009) With the old concrete now removed, the steel beams framing the workman brace up the pier where the new concrete will rest. The size of the workman against the steelwork gives a vivid picture of the scale of the project.

Today at one hundred years of age the Moodna Viaduct is famous for its length and longevity. But more than a hundred miles away and more than a half century older stands **(below)** another of the Erie's celebrated engineering wonders, the stone arched, 1200 foot long, Starrucca Viaduct. Opened in 1848, two years before the opening of both the Newburgh branch and the Erie mainline itself. The Viaduct was built by James P. Kirkwood who told the Erie officials he could span this quarter mile wide valley as long as cost was no object. Three other contractors had already walked away. Under great pressure to meet their construction deadlines, the officials agreed.

Employing stone from a quarry three miles away and a work force of 800 men, the Viaduct was opened in a year's time and in 1848 dollars cost $320.000. The viaduct was the most expensive railroad bridge in the world at that time. Engineer Kirkwood was another of a long line of Erie Engineers who would go on to gain worldwide acclaim for their work*. While the Erie had a structure that is still in service to this day, outliving the Erie itself and as sturdy and as breathtaking a sight as the day it opened. *

—*From "Between the Ocean and the Lakes--The story of the Erie"—by Edward Harold Mott—1899

Railfan.net photo, Fred Stratton

Returning to the Newburgh branch: New Windsor to Washingtonville

(Top) New Windsor station, midway between Newburgh and Vails Gate **(Below)** Vails Gate Jct. Starting from Vails Gate, the Erie's two Newburgh branches formed a triangle with the section of the Erie mainline between Greycourt and Harriman *Both pictures, Glenn T. Marshall*

Vails Gate Jct. had several crossover switches plus the switch to the shortcut branch, all hand thrown. Around the 1920's the switch tender had bad feet so he used a bicycle to go back and forth to line the switches for movement through the Jct.

Timetable direction on all ERIE branches was eastbound to the Mainline and Westbound to the stub end. The crossovers were considered the end of double track from Newburgh and from there east to Rt.94 the second track was considered a siding. Movements from Newburgh would go thru the crossovers in front of the station and then move over the highway and take either the Shortcut or the Greycourt line.

Late one night, with no switch tender on duty, a crew off the extra board with a light engine from Newburgh didn't stop and go through the crossovers, but continued on until they hit the derail at Vails Gate and turned over. I believe the fireman was killed. The coal from the tender was visible down the bank for years afterwards.

About 1914 Russell Havens was firing the local passenger that made three trips in fourteen hours over the Branch. On one trip they picked up milk cars at Washingtonville. Leaving Salisbury Mills the Brakeman in full uniform would ride the back tender step in order to cut the engine off as soon as they stopped in Washingtonville. The idea was to cut the engine off quickly, pick up the milk and leave on time. They only had three minutes for the stop. The problem was the creamery was a facing point switch so the engine would nose in get the milk cars back out and shove them up the main across the highway crossing. The Brakeman would hold them with a handbrake.

The engine would go into the creamery siding, the fireman would throw the switch and the brakeman would drop the milk cars by using the handbrake. The engine would come out put the train together and head for Greycourt.

Dennis Carpenter

Just beyond mile marker G14, to the right of the track in the distance, is where Vails Gate station once stood. The connection to the line to Greycourt was where the old switch ties trail off towards the bottom of picture. And what is now an industrial spur was once the line running from Vails Gate to Harriman by way of Enderlin, Mountainville, Woodbury, Highland Mills and Central Valley.

The line's direct route between Newburgh and the Erie mainline at Harriman, as opposed to the more roundabout trip to Greycourt and then down the Newburgh branch, gave the line the nickname the "short cut". The shortcut was built in a year's time and was opened with the laying of the last rail on July 13, 1869*. Opening ceremonies came that August.

The Greycourt line had its opening ceremonies on January 8, 1850*. More than one hundred years later, opening ceremonies long since forgotten, a certain (very) young author would see his first train here and the only train he would ever see on the Greycourt Line.

*From "The next station will be"
Railroadainians of America   1986

The roadbed of the short cut today runs alongside the New York State Thruway almost all the way into Mountainville, where the Thruway crosses over the former roadbed.

(Below) Railroad culvert, just east of Vails Gate Junction

(Above and bottom) Long before Vail's gate's rise and fall as a busy railroad junction, it was a center of activity in America's war for American independence. Washington's Headquarters, Knox's Headquarters and The Edmonston house **(Below)** are all just a few short miles from the Army's last encampment, and only ten miles from West Point.

After passing under the Thruway, we cross on the Greycourt line Rt. 94, and what was once the site of a second Vails gate station. (Picture unavailable)

Once past Rt. 94 we pass mile marker G13. About a mile ahead the roadbed now passes behind a modern high school, altering the scenery, and marker G13 is gone. (2008)

But way back when it was from here a fair two miles of walking along an uphill grade and a long "S" curve through the surrounding hillside before the farmlands of Salisbury Mills started to appear. (Mileposts G13 to G11)

Roadbed, just past Rt. 94

(Above) G13   **(Below)** Roadbed, going away from Vails Gate

A contrast in time: An old railroad telegraph
pole with the new school (barely discernable)
in the background

Leaving Vails Gate, the r-o-w will start to head into the first of the long turns, this one on a high embankment. It's the start of the uphill grade before the Erie crosses over the line of the New York, Ontario and Western Railway. (O&W) USGS map

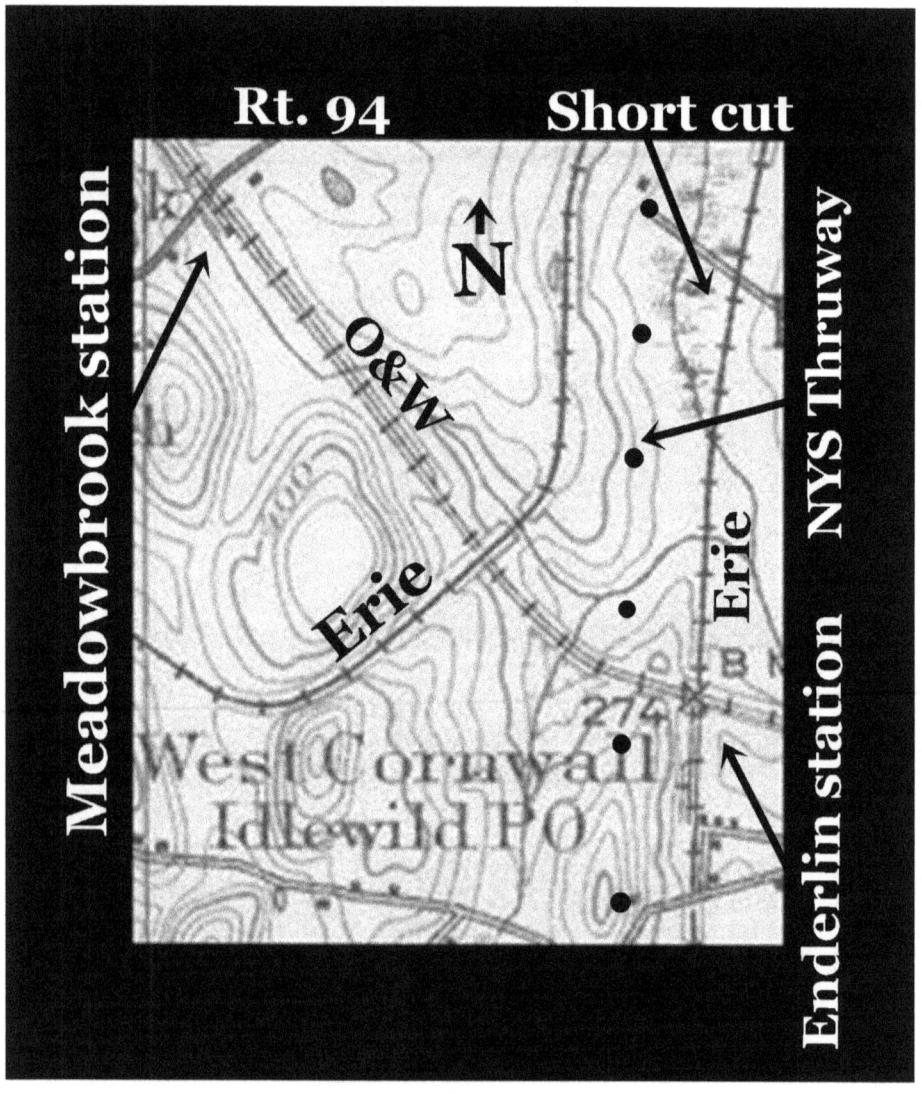

In the picture above, the roadbed of the O&W railroad passes below the Erie's line to Greycourt. We are looking north, in the direction of the Meadowbrook station. About a mile behind us, the O&W will duck under the Thruway before passing over a short bridge above the shortcut.

The Erie's shortcut was opened just months after the golden spike ceremony that opened America's very first transcontinental railroad on May 10, 1869. Up until the early 1880's the Erie would enjoy a monopoly on being the only direct railroad line to the bustling, Hudson River port city of Newburgh. (Con't next page)

With the building of The West Shore Railroad through Newburgh at the same time as the building of the O&W, the opening of the Poughkeepsie railroad bridge and the era of Maybrook rail yard just over the horizon, the building boom that would become known as "Railroad fever" was in full swing.

> What was it the engines said?
> Pilots touching head to head
> Two engines facing on a single track
> Half a world behind each back

From an observer at the opening of the Transcontinental railroad

We will come back later to take a proper look at the O&W and the shortcut. Right now, let's continue along the Newburgh branch to Salisbury Mills.

*About a quarter mile past the O&W, Erie bridge, mile marker G12 can still be found on the Erie. Toppled and broken, but still where an Erie work crew set it so long ago.

Coming into Salisbury Mills
The crossing of the Erie and the O&W at Meadowbrook is in the upper right hand corner.

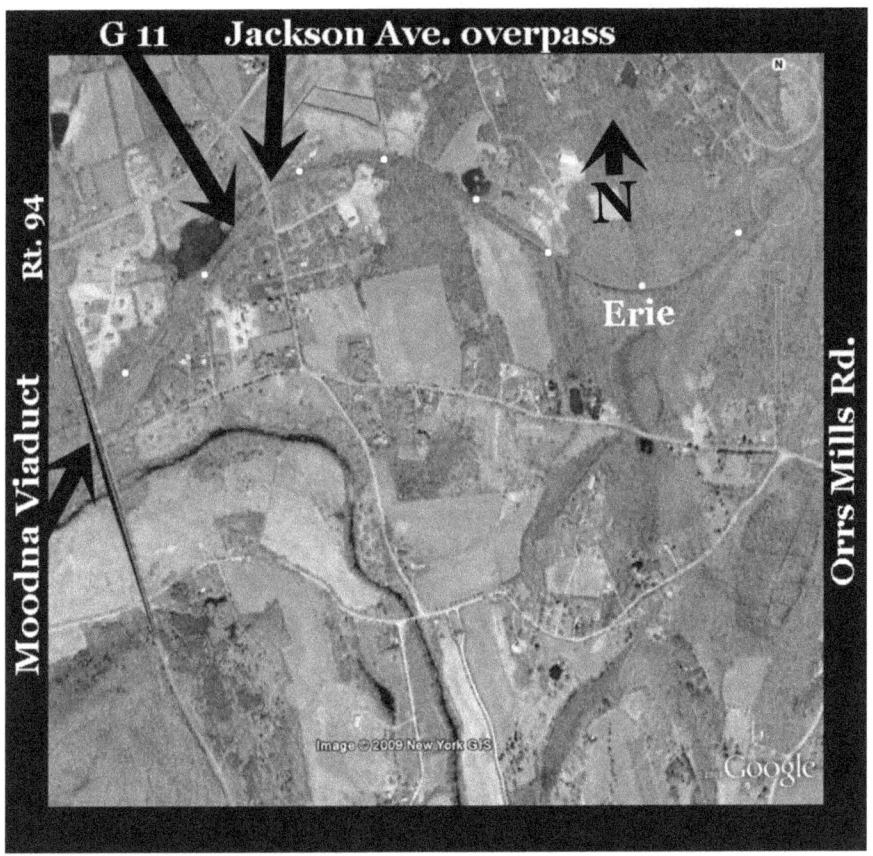

Image C. 2009 New York GIS

The Jackson Avenue overpass in the summer of 1985
The Erie name was still on the abutment below.

Imagine at this now quiet place the ground bearing down under hundreds of tons of approaching metal; the pitch changing as the ground turns into the openness of the bridge. The "ta-tumm-ta tumm, ta-tumm-ta tumm" of wheels on rail joints. Whistle and caboose fade into the distance....

The overpass site today

When the Jackson Avenue overpass was removed, a nearby house got some of the abutment stones for a kind of fence/sculpture. The town garage got the rest for a platform base.

Frost covers the ground near marker G11 on a cold October morning

Roadbed looking back towards Jackson Avenue

(Above) Salisbury Mills
Orrs Mills Road runs through the center, while Rt. 94 is off to the right. Image C. 2009 Digital Globe

(Top) A railfan excursion on the branch **(Front cover picture)**
Harry Zannie photo, Russell Hallock collection
(Below) The same vantage point today

Savoir or Grim Reaper: A Conrail freight passes high overhead

Old Rt. 45 (Present day Rt.94) tunnel at the end of the Viaduct

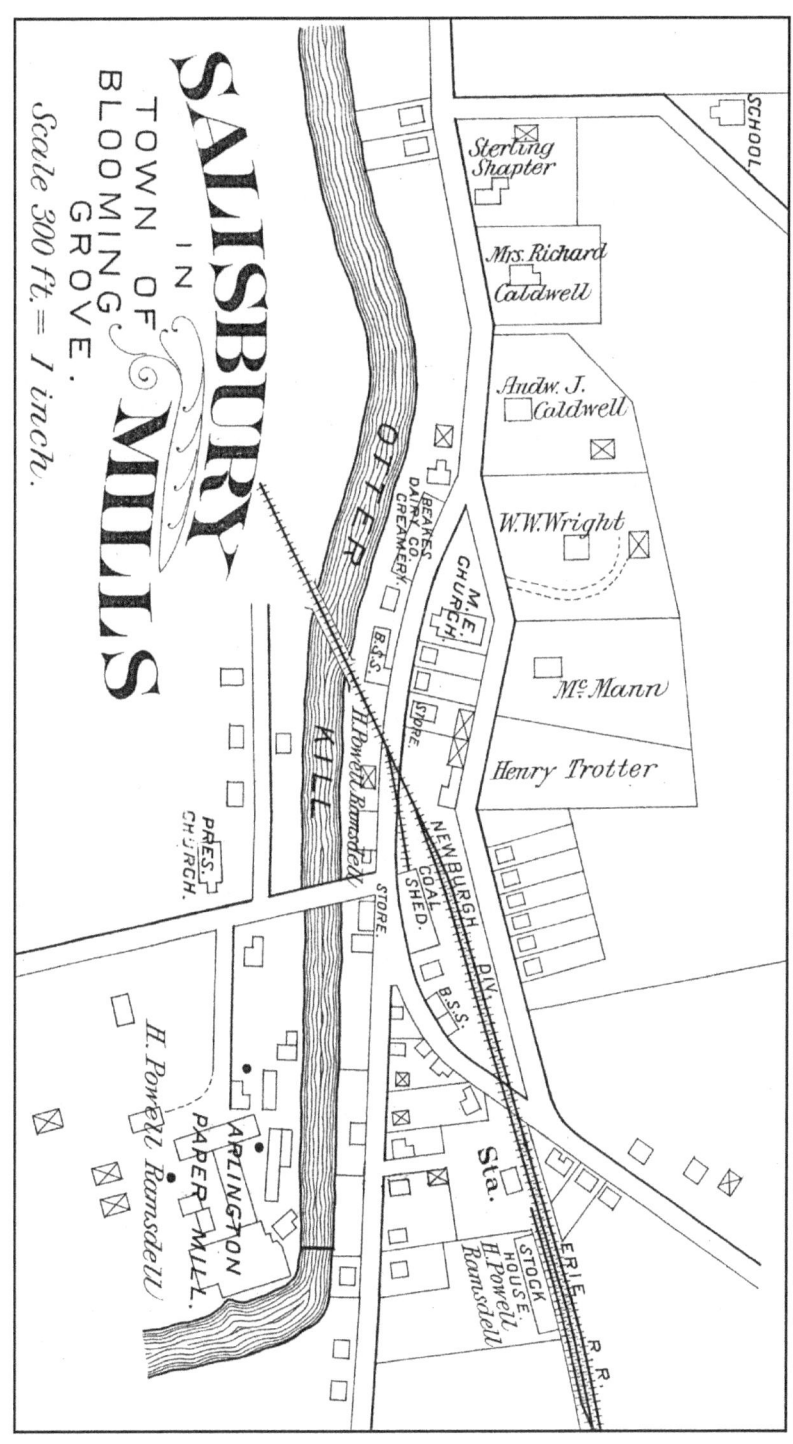

Map, last page, 1903 Orange County Atlas
By the beginning of the 1900's the name Murderer's creek was fading into history. The USGS map for 1902 name the entire length of the creek as Moodna while the map from the Orange County Atlas calls this stretch Otter Kill, one of the creeks main feeder streams.

Two memorials to three wars stand between
the Clove and Orrs Mills Grade crossings.
(Pages 80-82)

Walter Kierzkowski

Clove Road crossing **(Inset)** Marker G10, a half mile to the right of Clove Road   It's funny how some things happen: Way back when there was a house next to the roadbed near marker G10 I hated going past because of their barking, growling dog. Recently I went past that house. The dog is gone, probably has been for some time now, and I found myself missing it.....

Clove Road crossing today, at a close examination, has one unique distinction. Not only are the rails still in the crossing (2008) but a row of the ties for the passing track are still in place. Making this the only place outside of Greycourt and Vails Gate where there is still evidence of a double track on the Newburgh branch.

Orrs Mills crossing

Both older pictures: Engine 437   1970's   *Walter Kierzkowski*

For a few years after the rails were pulled a trackside phone box remained in place just past the Clove Road crossing, and the Orrs mills crossing sign lay alongside the crossing in the weeds.

Counting from the small railroad bridge over Cromline creek, one of the points of origin of the Moodna near Greycourt, the Newburgh branch will cross the waters of the Moodna six times. Moodna will also pass under the Erie's Moodna Viaduct, and the O&W's Orrs mills trestle. Lastly passing under the West Shore Railroad, at the point where the Moodna joins the Hudson River.

(Below) A few feet from the Orrs Mills crossing, we will cross over the first Moodna Bridge. Then about a half-mile ahead comes the second Moodna crossing and marker G9. Beyond that, we pass over a masonry culvert and a farmer's crossing **(Back cover picture)** before making another curve through the hillside.

Second Moodna bridge, looking back towards Salisbury Mills

After passing marker G8, we pass over several grade crossings before the third Moodna crossing coming into Washingtonville.

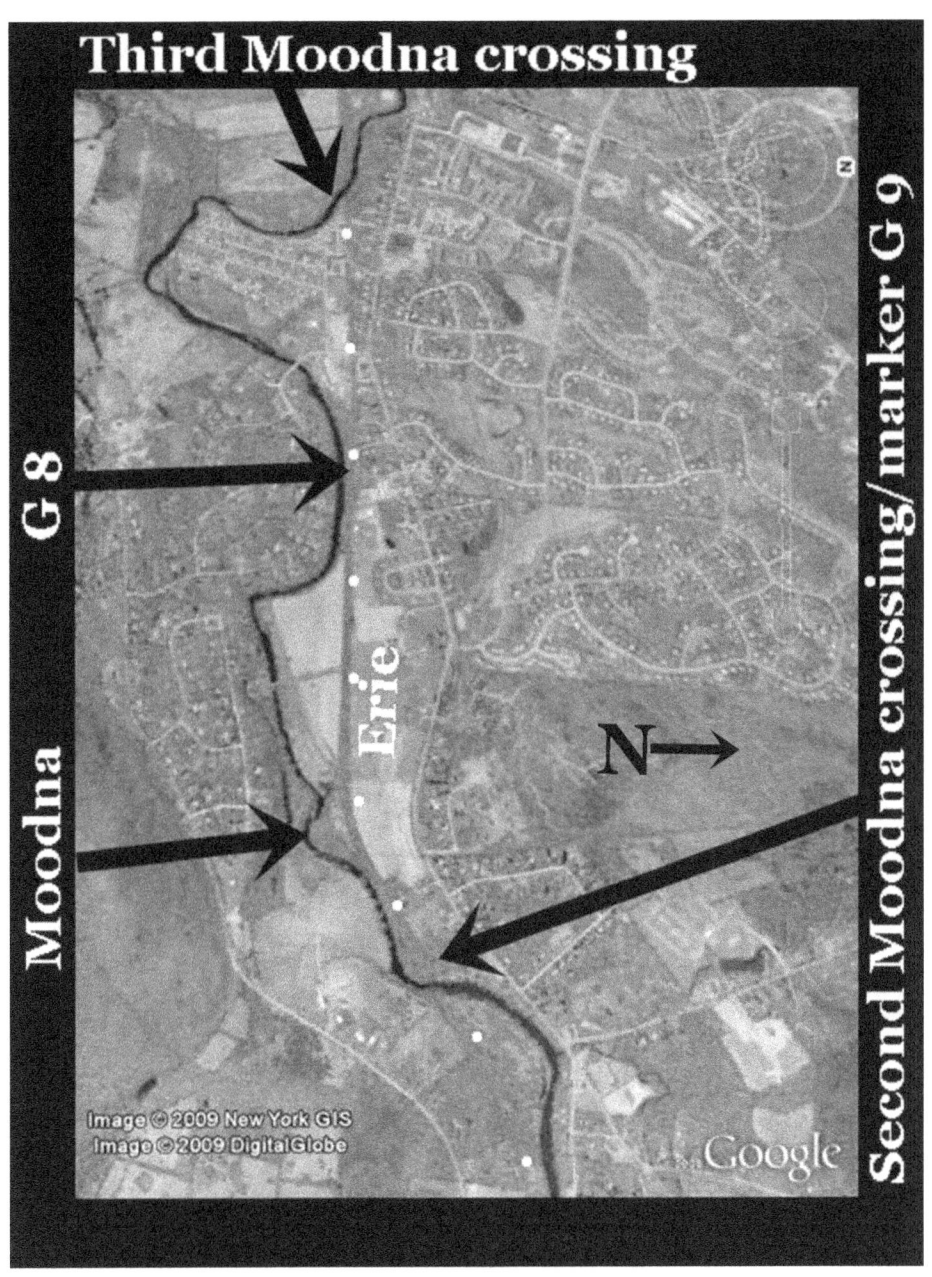

Image C. 2009 New York GIS   Image C. 2009 Digital Globe

The third Moodna Bridge, looking towards Washingtonville

Like a greeting from an old friend…………..

A sign left from the days when Edward and Joan McLaughlin ran an antique and book store out of the Washingtonville depot

Washingtonville, N.Y.

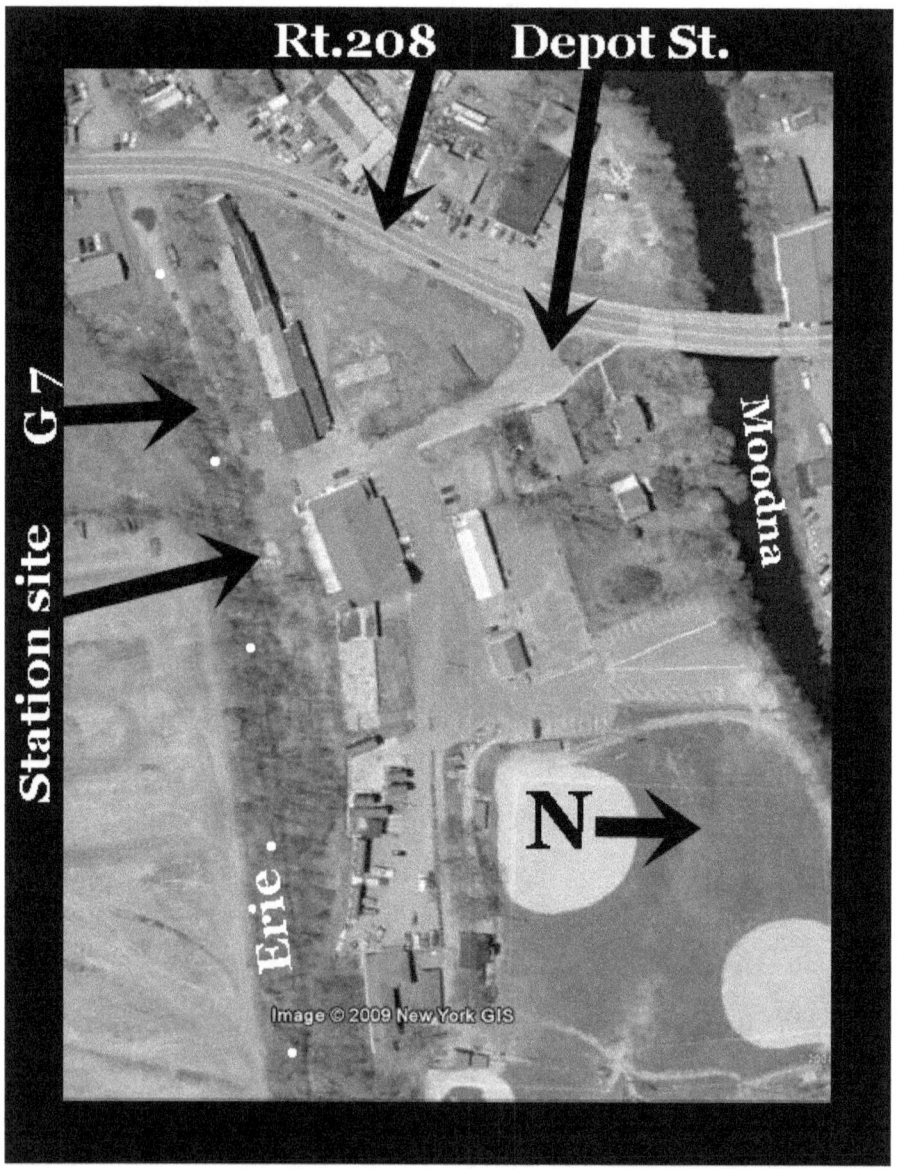

Brotherhood Winery, Washingtonville, N.Y.

(Above) Across from the Winery, one of Washingtonville's grand houses

Next three pages: *Tiffany windows, Moffat Library*

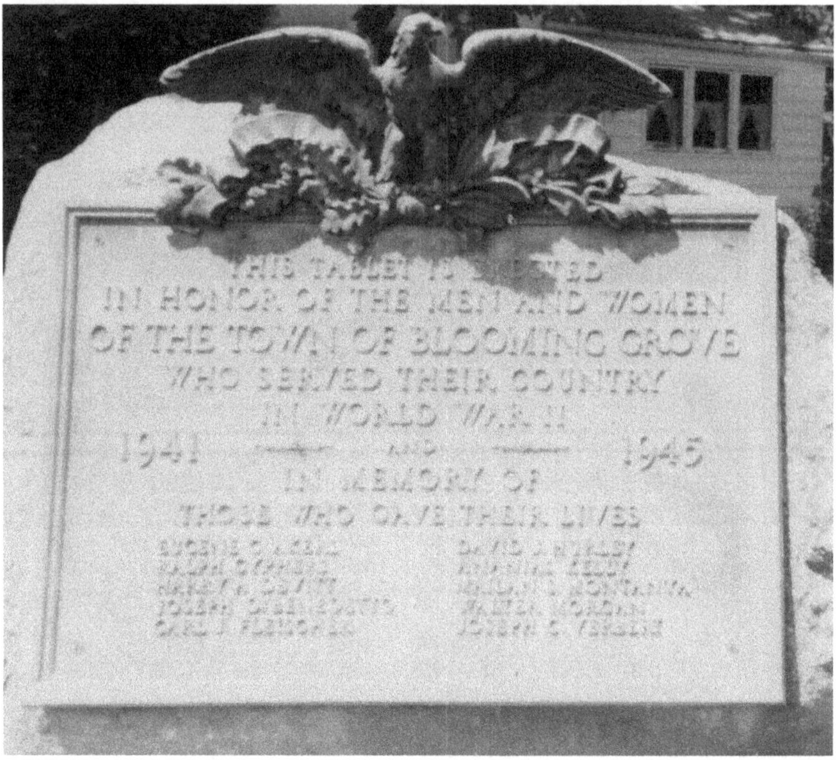
IN HONOR OF THE MEN AND WOMEN
OF THE TOWN OF BLOOMING GROVE
WHO SERVED THEIR COUNTRY
IN WORLD WAR II
1941 AND 1945
IN MEMORY OF
THOSE WHO GAVE THEIR LIVES

IS ERECTED
OF THE TOWN OF BLOOMING
WHO SERVED THEIR COUNTR
IN THE WORLD WAR
1917 AND 1919
IN MEMORY OF
THOSE WHO GAVE THEIR LIVES

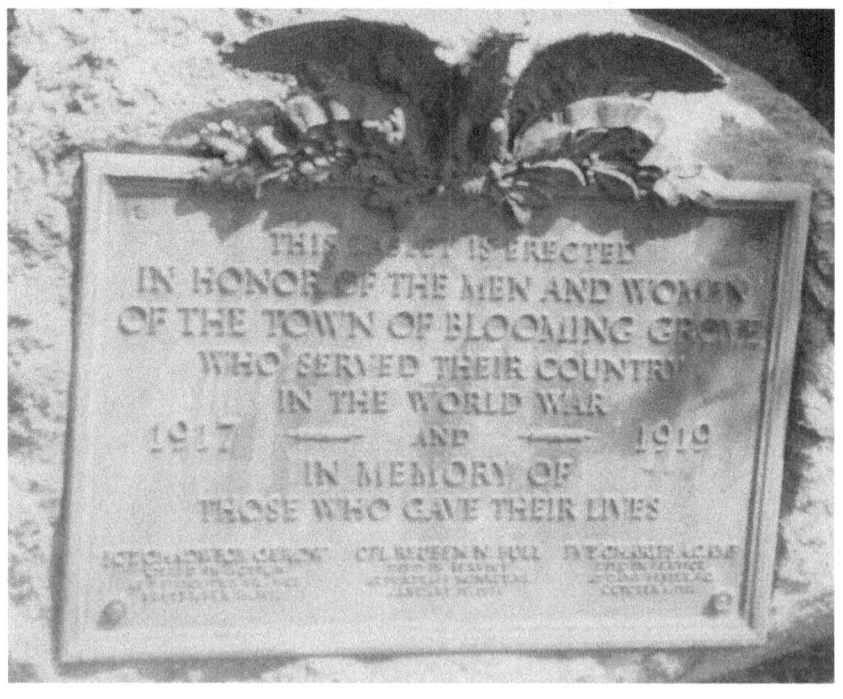

Marker along Rt. 94

With fife and drum I marched away, I could not heed what she did say, I'll not be back for many a day. Johnny has gone for a soldier

Pages 80-82: Two memorials to three wars, Salisbury Mills

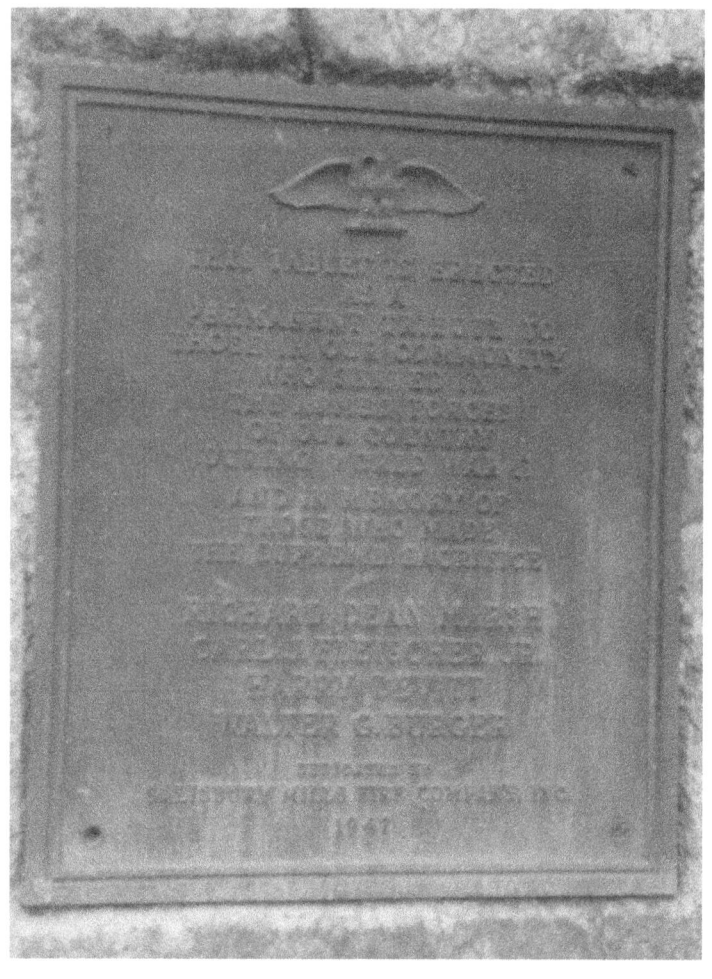

Washingtonville to Greycourt and beyond

July, 1964   *Dennis Carpenter*

Leaving Washingtonville, we cross the waters of the Moodna two more times. The fourth Moodna crossing Comes up fast after the Rt. 208 crossing

Blake Tatar

Fourth Moodna bridge

Just past the fourth bridge, near the Rt.94 crossing, was Borden's Creamery. The building survives but the chimney with the Borden name on it, now gone, was similar to the chimney that stands in Firthcliffe (Next page) at the former Firth Carpet Company. On a personal note, my family watched as youths the Firth chimney being put up. While at Borden's I watched history being taken down-a one brick at a time proposition.

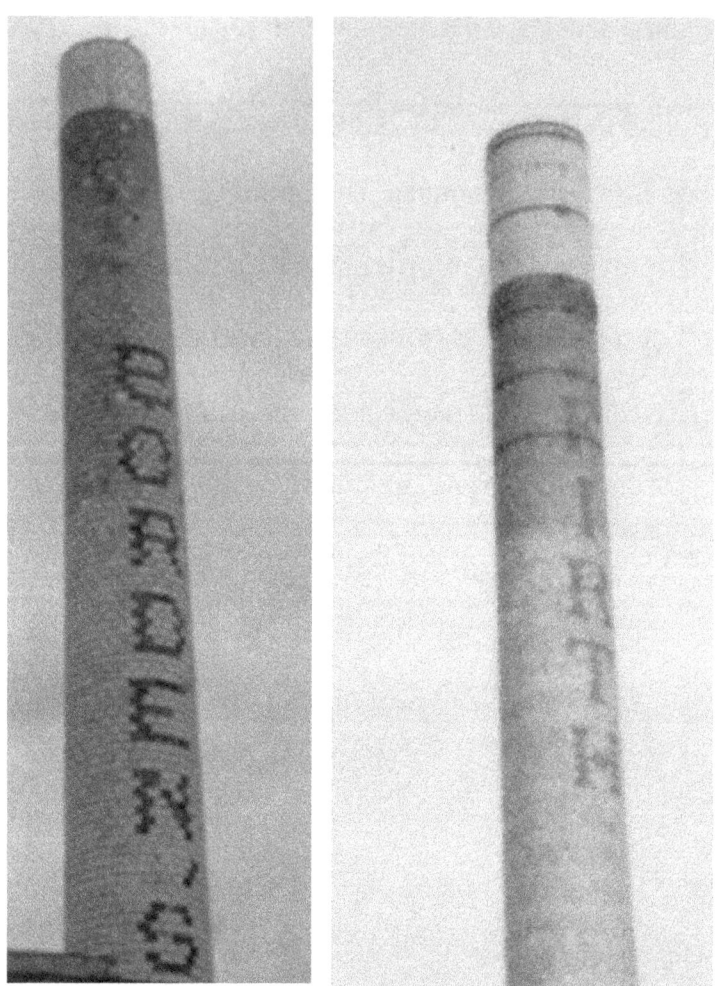

    My Grandfather, Fred Carpenter, was the engineer on the passenger back around WW I. He was shoving the milk up the main at Bordens and started into the siding when he saw the brakeman had a bad hand brake on the milk cars and couldn't hold them. He could have cleared the main with the engine but decided to stop and block it so the cars wouldn't roll on down to the Station and hit the passenger cars. When they hit everything went off the track but the engine did not roll over.

Dennis Carpenter

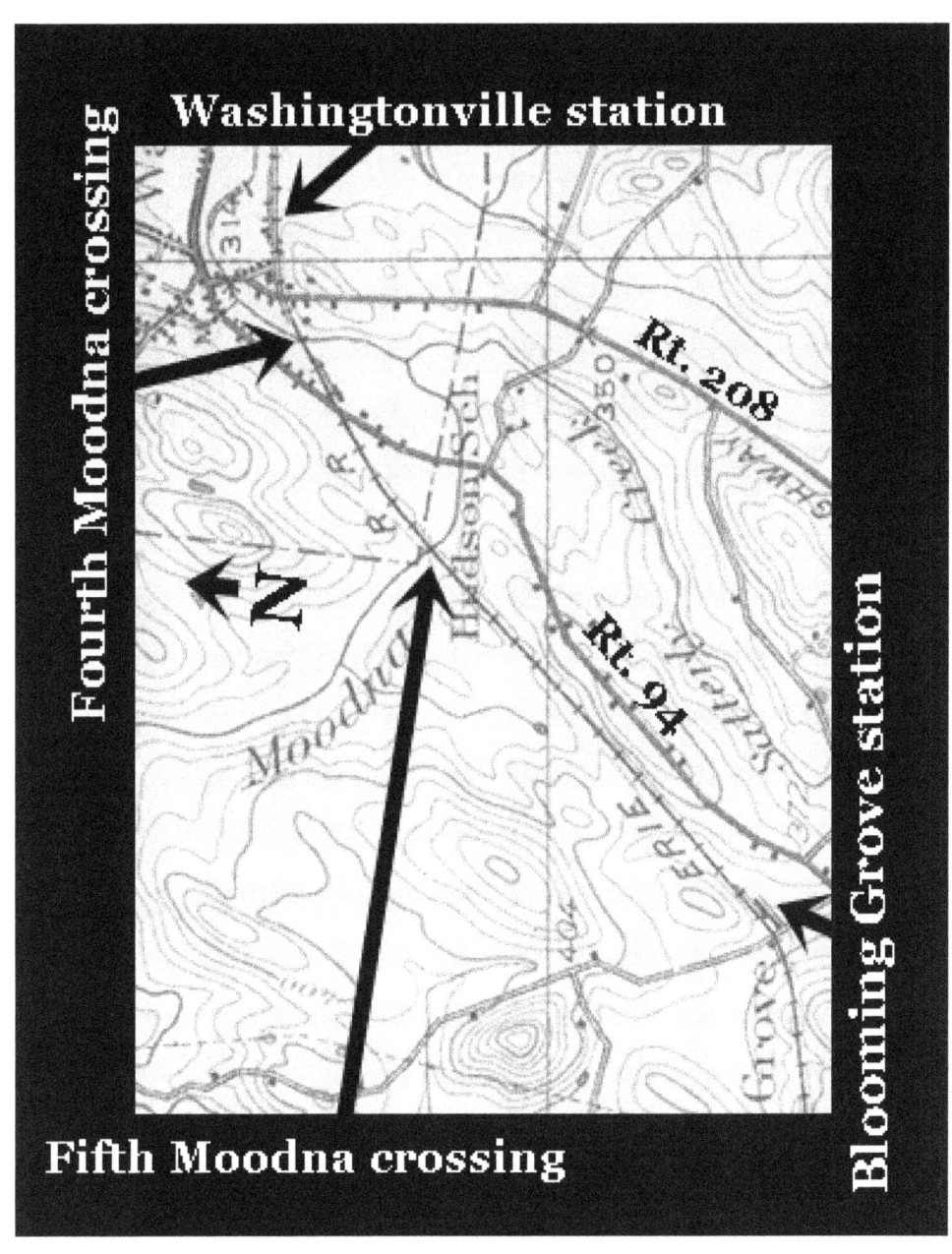

USGS map

87

Roadbed past Rt. 94   We are between mileposts 7 and 6 and coming up on the fifth Moodna bridge. Between mileposts 6 and 5 we will come up on Blooming Grove station.

(Top and bottom) The fifth Moodna bridge

What was once known as "Tin Bridge" because the original wooden bridge was clad in metal for fireproofing. *Edward McLaughlin*

(Above) Top of Tin Bridge- Both 1990

Dennis Carpenter

Back around 1990, when I was first working on Country Cousins, I made three trips over the Erie above Washingtonville. For some reason on the section above Blooming Grove I was always glad to get back across tin bridge (see Icabod Crane) and never understood why. Sometime after, I became involved in a conversation with someone who had a few memories to share about the Erie track above Washingtonville. Well, without me bringing it up, I was told that out in the woods, along the old railroad line above Washingtonville, "something" was out there.........You can't make this stuff up...

Above Tin Bridge, the roadbed has in sections fallen into a poor state of repair.

Station, Blooming Grove, N. Y.

Blooming Grove station   No longer standing
Walter Kierzkowski

Marker along Rt. 94 near Blooming Grove station

(**Above**) Marker G4, looking back towards Blooming Grove   (**Below and next page**)
The roadbed here is coming out of the last of the long turns. And from here it's a virtual straight run into Greycourt.

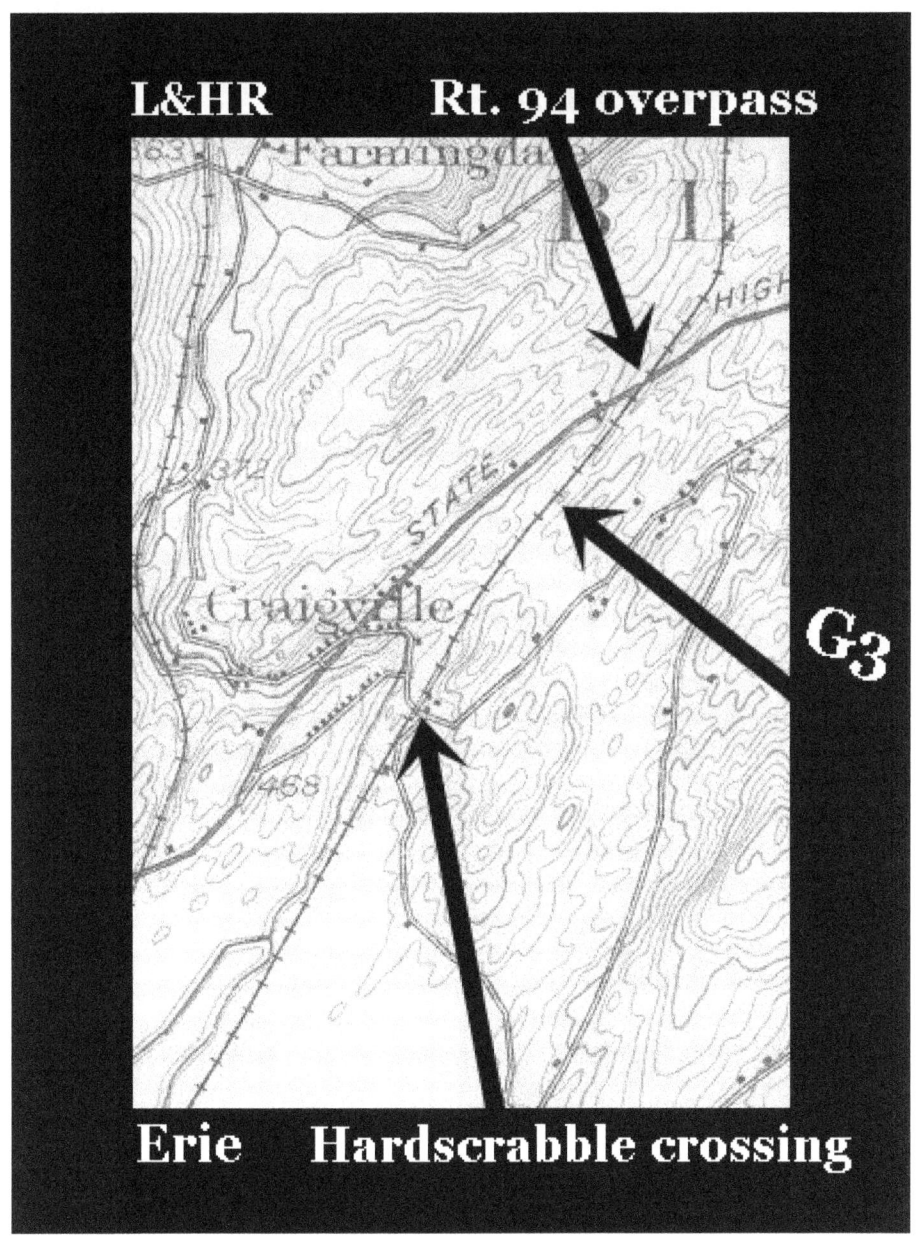

USGS map

Rt.94 overpass, looking back towards Blooming Grove

A Photographer gets caught in the picture.

Looking towards the 3 miles of straightaway into Greycourt

Imagine standing here when you could already see the smoke and hear the whistle of an engine up above Craigville. An afternoon thunderstorm is rolling in and the distant whistle seems to be answering the thunder back. Up at Craigville station the boards are green and the headlight draws ever closer, the smoke and sound of exhaust ever thicker. Above the rumble of hundreds of tons of moving steel that grows ever louder the whistle blows for the bridge. Then just as fast as it came the whistle, smoke and flying side rods vanish around the curve behind us.

That abutment on the Rt. 94 bridge was home to a very large Blacksnake. Let's just say neither of us knew the other was there when we met -"briefly"!

When I last saw it back in 1990, the whistle post for Hardscrabble crossing (Craigville) was facing more to the ground than the tracks and marker G3* had fallen over. *Marker G6 and G3 are now off the roadbed in private hands. *Russell Hallock*

Rock cut past Rt. 94, looking back towards the overpass

Craig: dictionary: *Scotland*; a rocky hill or mountain

Edward McLaughlin's "Around the watering through" gives a much more complete and colorful history of Craigville and it's namesake, Scottish born, John Craig, than could be attempted within these pages.

Hardscrabble crossing, looking into the last of the rock cuts
Back in 1990 the rails were still in the crossing. Craigville station site is behind us, but unrecognizable. **(Next page)** crossing site, 2008
Is that the rails still showing through the newer pavement?

Craigville station   *Walter Kierzkowski*

Just past Hardscrabble crossing we pass through the last of the rock cuts then it's a straight run for the last two miles into Greycourt and we enter the famous black dirt region. The richness of the black dirt is not only famous for what it helps to grow, but also what it preserves. I was looking for a picture that could best describe the richness of the black dirt just as this picture appeared **(Bottom)** in the newspaper of a prehistoric Moose Elk that was recovered from the rich soil that had preserved it for over 11,000 years.

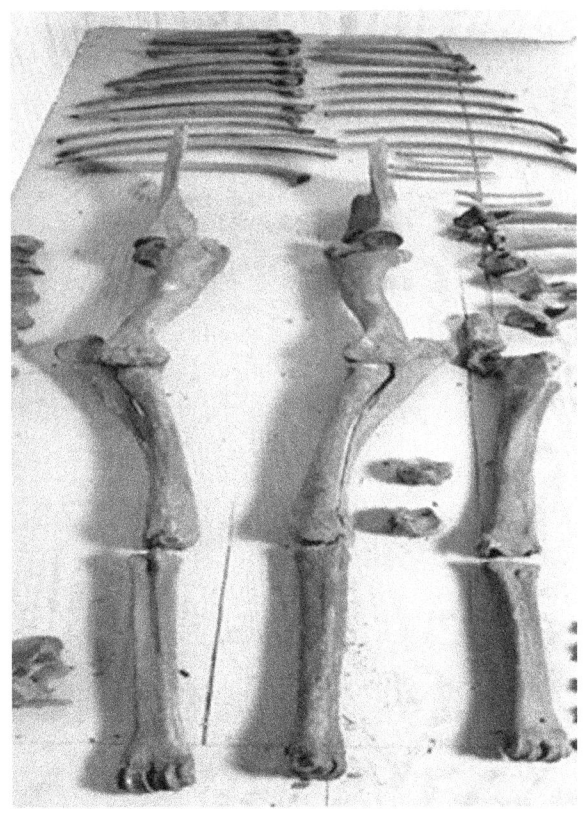

The rich soil that is so great for farming and preservation was also a nightmare for the builders of the Erie Railroad who had to create a stable roadbed by sinking a network of wooden piles in the ground to make a trestle-like framework, and then spend years after filling in soil around it to make the stable roadbed we recognize today. **(Below)** coming into Greycourt

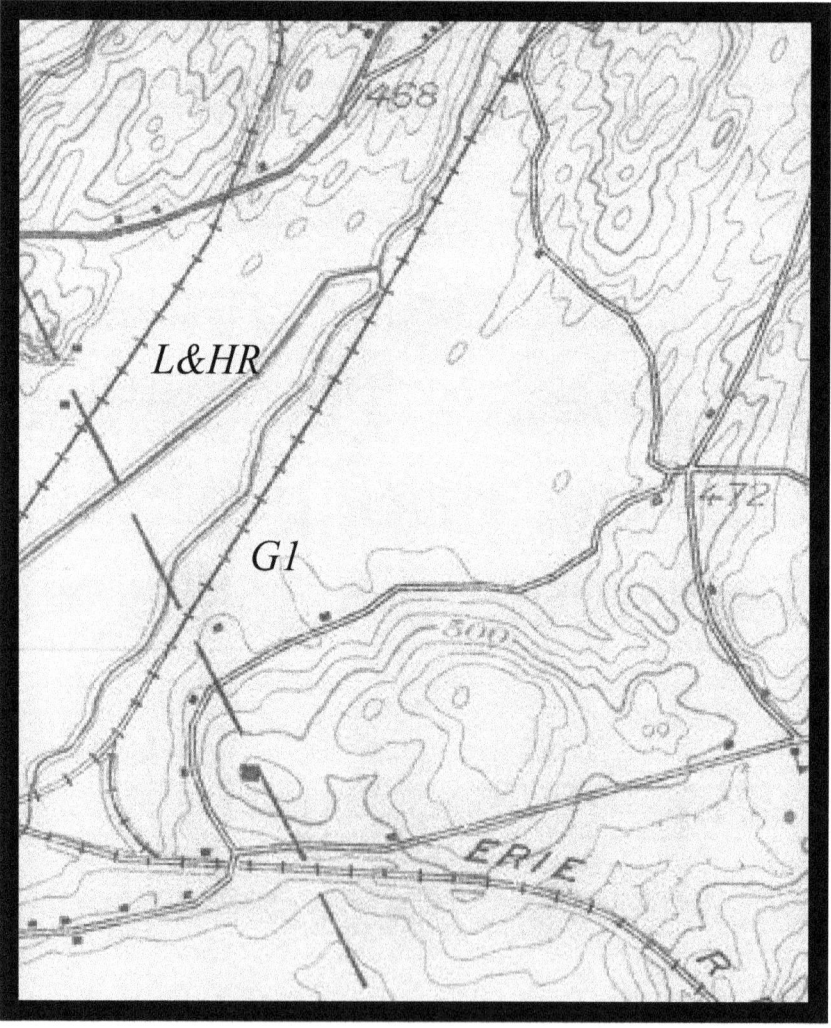

(Above and below) These two pairs of bridges are the last crossings on the branch before coming into Greycourt. We are on the "Northbound" leg of the wye heading in the direction of the site of Greycourt station.

(Above) The wye is to the left, the former mainline track is off to the far right, visible through the brush. Running between them on the former roadbed is today's Orange County's Heritage trail. **(Bottom)** JC 53 (Jersey City 53) at midpoint on the wye

(Above) The "Southbound" leg of the wye
USGS map

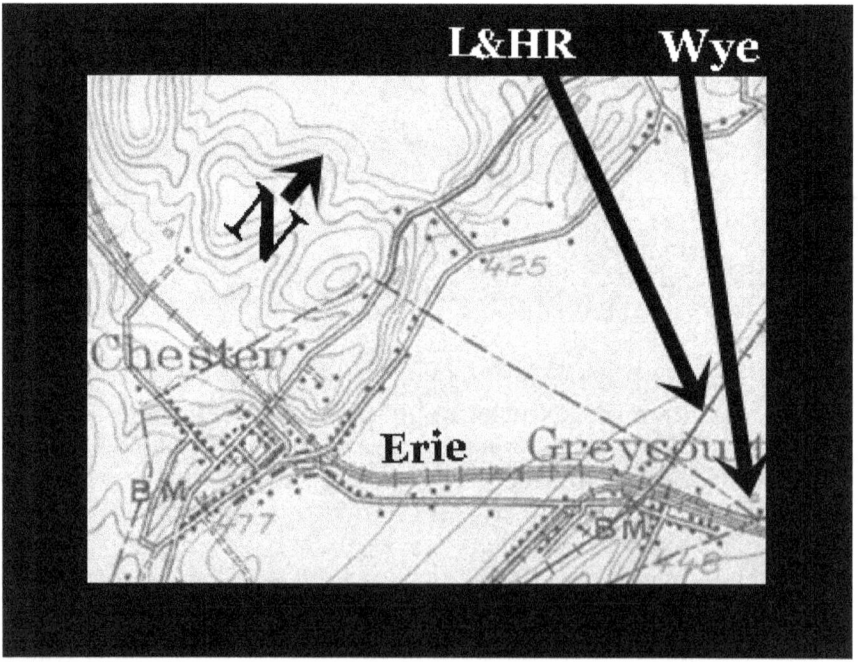

Greycourt, N.Y.

Greycourt station stood to the left in the bottom picture. The Leigh and Hudson River R.R. bridge is visible in the background behind the station.

(Top) *Chester Historical society*

1967 Dennis carpenter

(Above) Greycourt, 1971 *Dennis carpenter*
(Below) the line coming from Greycourt connects with the former L&HR at Hudson Junction

The construction of the line from Greycourt to Newburgh was begun by the proposed Hudson and Delaware Railroad in the 1830's. The H&D defaulted on it's initial charter and after years of financial and political wrangling the Newburgh branch was finished by the Erie Railroad in 1850.* Freight cars could now be taken to Newburgh and then ferried across the Hudson River to points west, mostly coal cars.

The opening in 1889-90 of the Poughkeepsie railroad bridge across the Hudson would end the car ferry service in Newburgh. At that same time, what was now the L&HR R.R. was extended from Hudson Junction to the connection with the O&W, and what was at the time the Central New England Railroad, at Maybrook. (Continued next page)

*Around the watering through   1994 by Edward McLaughlin

The Railroad names and the names of the players behind the stage were in constant change, but the interchange that was to become massive Maybrook yard had begun. Up until the 1880's, the L&HR, originally built as the Warwick Valley RR, ended here at Greycourt.

(Left) Ancient crossbuck near Hudson Jct.

(Right) marker G10 (Maybrook 10)

 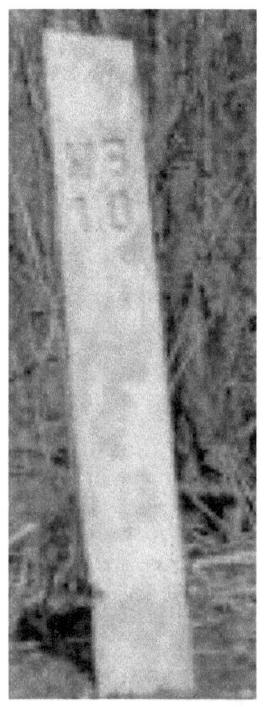

Next pages: The former Erie mainline becomes part of the rails to trails movement.

When in my sunrise years, barely a teen
I had a friend in the Erie Railroad when her rails still had their young sheen
I heard her at sunrise, I heard her at night
I heard her amid storms and knew all was all right
I could run alongside the Erie back in the days before war would leave my youth on some distant shore
My sunrise years have all passed, my health is now frail
What I knew as the Erie my grandchildren know as a trail
There is a place where the rails can still be seen, there in the bushes, without their young sheen
Come my last sunrise I will take the Lord's hand
And I and the Erie will be young once again.

The Erie mainline-Today's Heritage trail

USGS maps Coming into Goshen
  Mile marker JC (Jersey City) 58 to the right

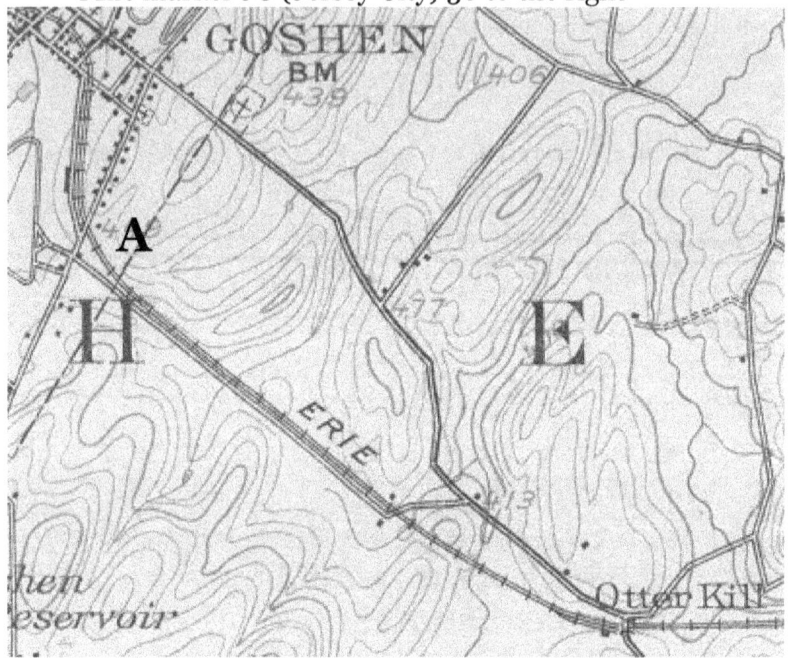

Back in 1991 this portion of the roadbed was all but
Inaccessible due to the overgrowth

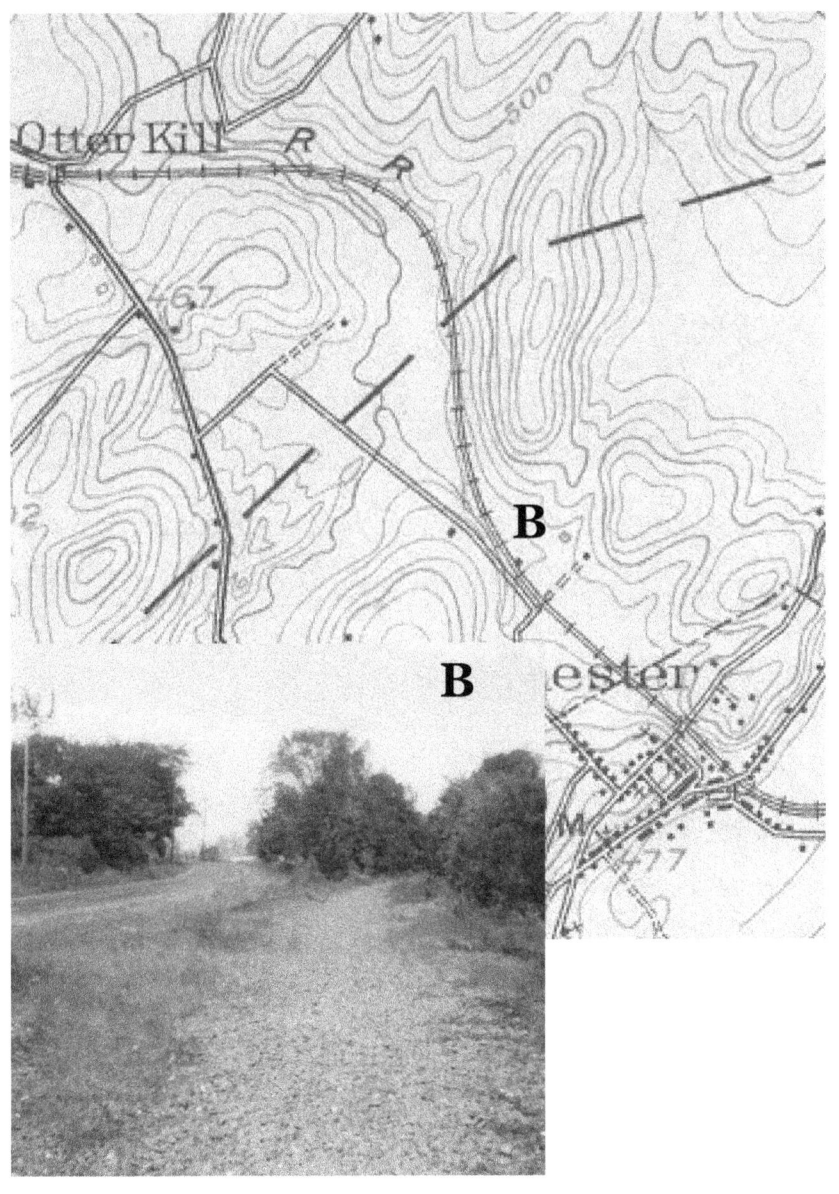

C
Chester
Greycourt
C
B M
477
B M
448

ERIE
D
R R
559
Oxford
HIGHWAY
D

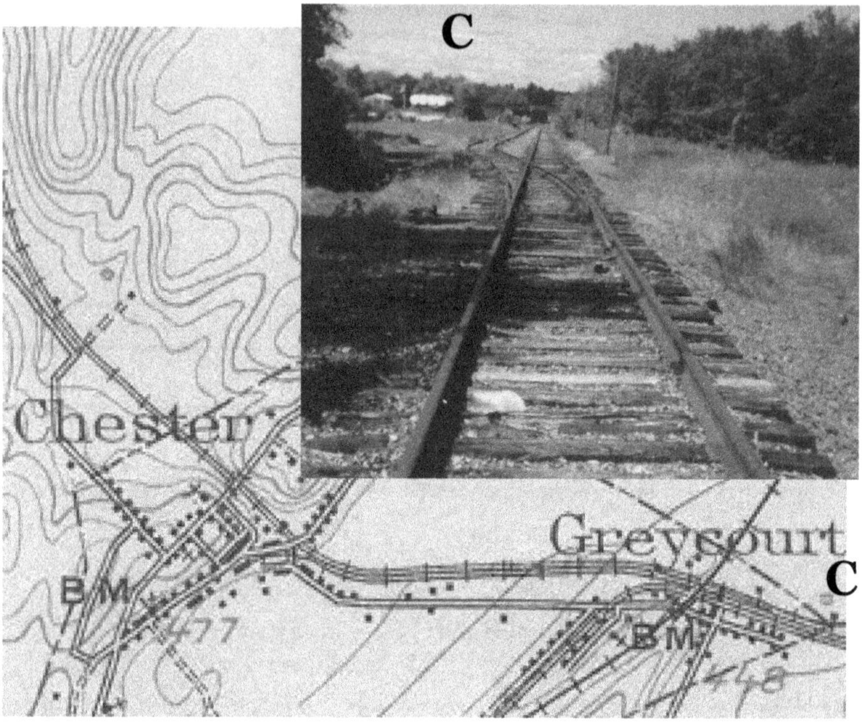

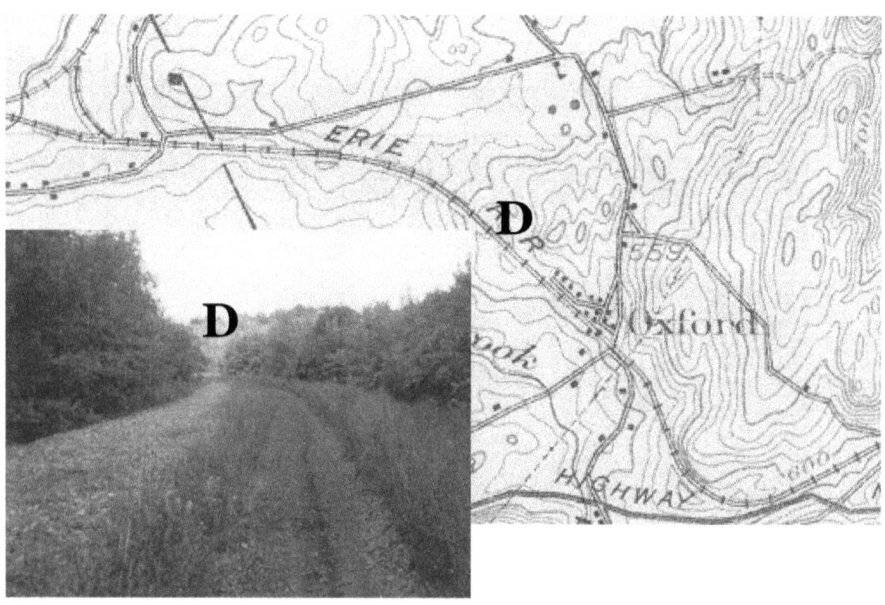

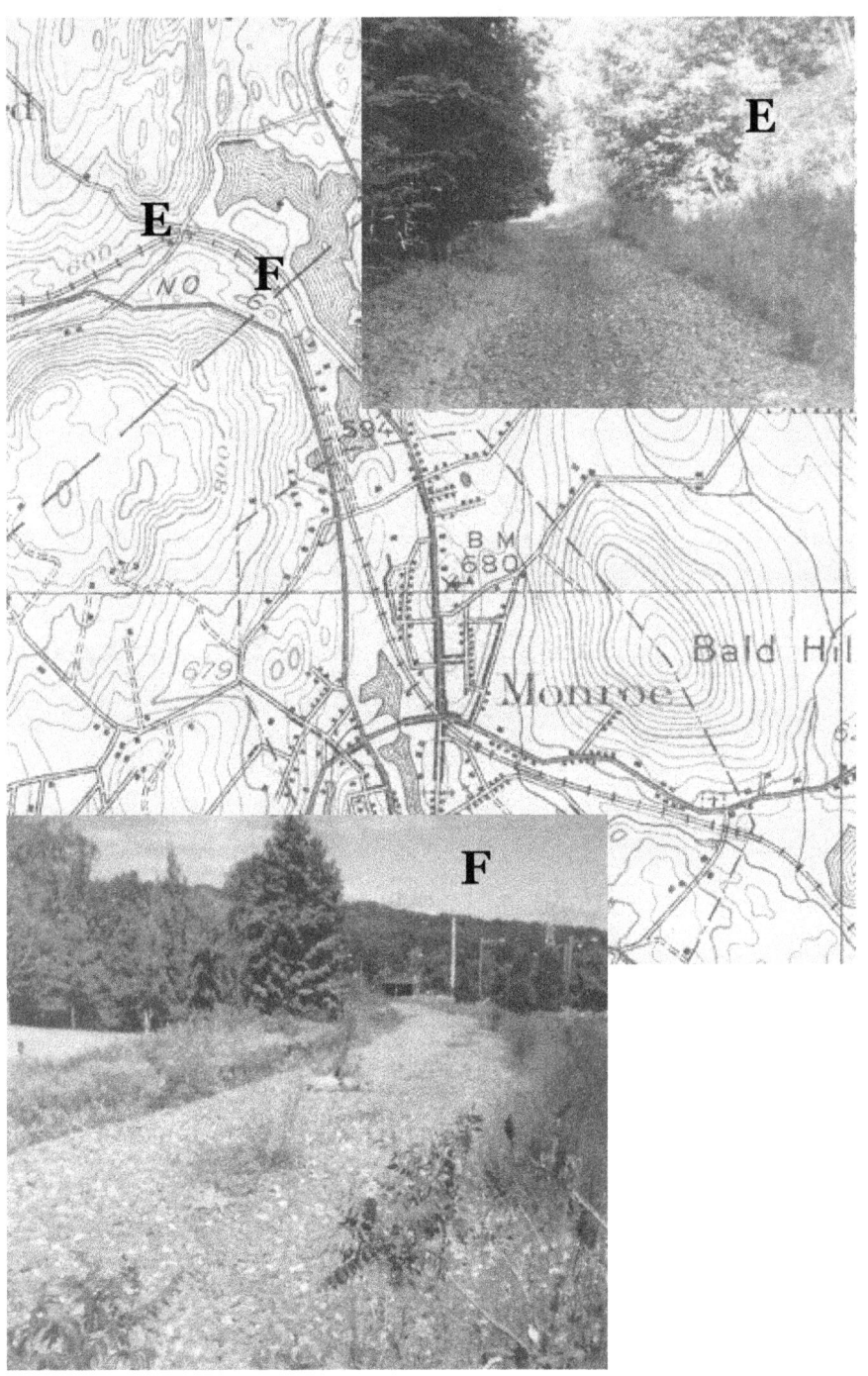

113

Epilogue: At last the Graham line gets the green light: *Excerpts from the Times-Herald Record, April 17, 1983*

New Hampton- Betty Bende and her daughter, Mary Ann Hite, dutifully tacked one last cardboard–and–crayon greeting to the Cheery tree that has been their signboard for years.

"It's not going to be the same, nothing is going to be going by here —isn't that a sin?" Mrs. Bende says, admiring the last of her poster size creations: Farewell from us.

For the past several years, the two New Hampton women have built a tradition of offering holiday greetings to trainmen passing on the main line tracks a few boxcar lengths from their Ryerson Road home. "It all started one day when I waved one at one of them; he waved back and we just kept it up," recalls Mrs. Hite".

The waving soon led to the signs, with the Ryerson Road family wishes for a "Merry Christmas", "Happy New Year" and even a few "Happy summers". Passing trainmen acknowledge the greetings with a few resounding hits of their locomotive's air horn. There have been exchanges of holiday gifts. The family has taken jars of home- grown fruits and vegetables to the train crews in Middletown and Goshen. And the family has found more than one bottle of holiday cheer lying alongside the rail crossing next to their home at Christmas.

The Bende-and later the Hite-families have lived in the stone house by the tracks for 48 years, ever since Mrs. Bende and her husband decided it would be a perfect retirement refuge from Brooklyn.

Mrs. Hite has grown up, Mrs. Bende told, listening to the daily reveille of passing freights and passenger trains.

All that changes as of today. The last main line train pulled into Middletown station at 5:59 P.M Saturday, marking an end of 142 years of passenger and freight service to the villages of Goshen, Chester, Monroe and Harriman. It will also start a new era of rail service to for rail stations in the town of Wallkill (Serving Middletown), Campbell Hall, Salisbury Mills-Cornwall, and a new Harriman station.

The switch comes as part of a state Department of Transportation plan five years ago to upgrade Conrail's Southern tier route-the former Erie Lackawanna line that crosses the state from Lake Erie to Binghamton and then drops south through Sullivan and Orange Counties.

The state agreed to spend $23 million improving the tracks in exchange for Conrail's promise to continue using the New York state route as a major freight link of the Great lakes states and New York City.

But the rail improvements encountered a snag just north of Middletown. The state insisted it only had enough money to upgrade only one route and left the choice of the main line or the Graham line to the county. Whichever was picked, the other would be abandoned.

Middletown officials had dreamed for a half century of ridding their downtown of the Erie Railway station and yard they coveted for Urban Renewal and they were the first to tout the wisdom of choosing the graham route. But Middletown's dream was a nightmare for communities and rail commuters farther down the main line passenger route.

Most of the commuters and the main line communities waged a 3 year legal and public relations battle against the Graham proposal that ended last summer with MTA's decision to accept the passenger train switch.

But some merchants in the main line villages are worried that the loss of the trains their communities also will spell a loss of hundreds of early morning customers. "Between five and seven in the morning, I probably go through 200 to 260 cups of coffee" says Ross Forman, owner of PJ's Cutting board deli, a block from the Monroe train station. In Goshen, Joy Marker is concerned about losing "a nice part of our business". Her tobacco shop and variety store on West Main Street within sight of the station has opened at 6:15 A.M. for years to cater to commuters   (Continued next page) who stopped for a newspaper, a pack of cigarettes or that last minute birthday card they forgot to buy the night before.

"I used to say these trains made my card displays dirty, especially when you leave the door open. Now I would be happy to have them back," Mrs. Marker says. "Were going to lose business and we'll lose a lot of friends too", she adds.

And up the line at Ryerson Road in the town of Wawayanda, Mrs. Hite has one less worry.

"The old cherry tree isn't going to last much longer, and I wasn't sure what we were going to hang the signs on", Mrs. Hite says. "I'm glad they're (the trains) going before us".

Peter Thompson, Staff Writer

From Goshen to Monroe, the former Erie mainline has become the Orange County Heritage trail. Plans are also in the works at the date of this writing (2009) to extend the Heritage trail west to Middletown and east to Harriman on the former roadbed. East of Greycourt, the roadbed starts the uphill grade to Monroe that was in the railroad's day called the Oxford Grade. Oxford Depot is midway on the grade. At the start of this uphill climb there is a section that I have come to call "the Grove" **(Below)** because in the summer there is nothing above you but trees and there is hardly a sound to be heard.

Diamond in the rough: Today's Heritage trail. That old signal post once guided trains coming down the Oxford grade. Today the trees and a chain link fence make the old signal post difficult to find except in the fall.

(Next page) Looking towards Greycourt
The bridge to the right now has a second life carrying bicyclers and walkers while the other two bridges are reverting back to nature.

Looking towards Greycourt

The Erie and her like are gone forever yes, but history itself has a way of coming full circle. Crowded highways, bottleneck airports and rising gas prices have caused ridership on Amtrak to increase to the point where for the first time in years (Continued next page)

Congress sees the wisdom of putting necessary money into improvements. And the sale of Conrail put the railroads in the northeast back in private hands. The work to refurbish the Graham line as a commuter necessity, a full twenty-five years ago now, was a sign of the railroad business in Orange County starting to climb back from the abyss.

View from Oxford grade, today's Heritage trail

My hopes are of the Greycourt line one day becoming rails to trails just like I once had hopes of it becoming a tourist railroad. If left alone some remnant of the bridges will always remain, but un-crossable. While nature will take back the right of way that the Erie "borrowed" from her for all those years.

Surely, lying somewhere out there on the right of way between Vails Gate and Greycourt, is a forgotten railroad spike that will lay there throughout the ages as a reminder of the days when America's future rode on a pair of iron rails.

Robert McCue

The New York, Ontario and Western Railroad, and the Erie's Newburgh "Short cut"

Having covered the Newburgh branch, we will now go back to Meadowbrook.

After passing underneath the Newburgh branch, going south from Meadowbrook, the O&W will first duck under the Thruway before passing over a small bridge above the shortcut at Enderlin.

The Enderlin station is still standing, but as private property. So lets take a moment here to look at what railroad stations that as of 2009 are still with us and some of the stations we have lost. All are monuments to a time when every town, great or small, tied its fortunes to being a stop on a railroad line.

We will begin by looking at the O&W's Meadowbrook station and sister Mechanicstown station before we travel down the line from Newburgh to Harriman. Then we will head up the Erie mainline to the Newburgh branch before returning to the O&W.

(Below) Abutment, O&W's bridge over the shortcut The Thruway bridge over the O&W is in the background.

(Above) The pride of the road: Engine 405 in her late 1930's "Streamstyled" finest passes Meadowbrook station and is about to duck under Rt. 45 (Present day Rt. 94). About a mile back the 405 passed over the Erie's "short cut", which by this time has already been abandoned. Now fast forward past ten years and an entire world war: The 405 has been scrapped, the O&W mainline has been single tracked and Meadowbrook station is about to be torn down. Another ten years beyond that, and the New York, Ontario and Western Railroad is now only a memory.

(Picture above) *Walter Kierzkowski*
Compare this picture with Mechanicstown station on the next page.

Mechanicstown station
Of all the O&W stations built between Cornwall and Middletown using this similar, but never exact, building pattern, the Mechanicstown is the last surviving sister.
(Next page) Trimwork, Mechanicstown station

A trip on the Erie shortcut

The Newburgh branch begins at the junction with the West Shore railroad at Newburgh.

Motorcar 4070 at Newburgh   *Russell Hallock*

New Windsor station site
Since this picture was taken, sometime back in the 1980's, this section of track between Newburgh and Vails Gate has been given a major overhaul.
Note the switch ties to the right.

(Above) Out of the curve and looking towards Vails Gate (2009)
(Below) The line to Greycourt breaks off to the left, the shortcut breaks off to the right

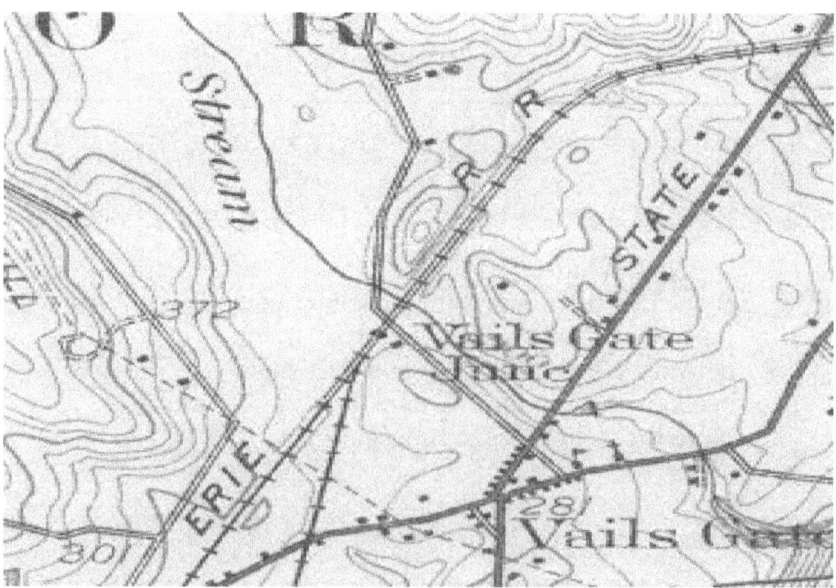

The coming of the O&W in the 1880's, and it's stations at Orrs Mills and Firthcliffe, ended Enderlin's days as a primary railroad station for Cornwall. On the 1902 map on the next page, Enderlin station is under the name "Idlewild P.O.". The name was an attempt by the Postal Service to avoid confusing West Cornwall with three other postal districts of Cornwall. The name Enderlin would not become official until 1909*.

Cornwall, N.Y. Images from the past, 1988   Friends of the Cornwall Public library

Enderlin station
Still standing (2009)

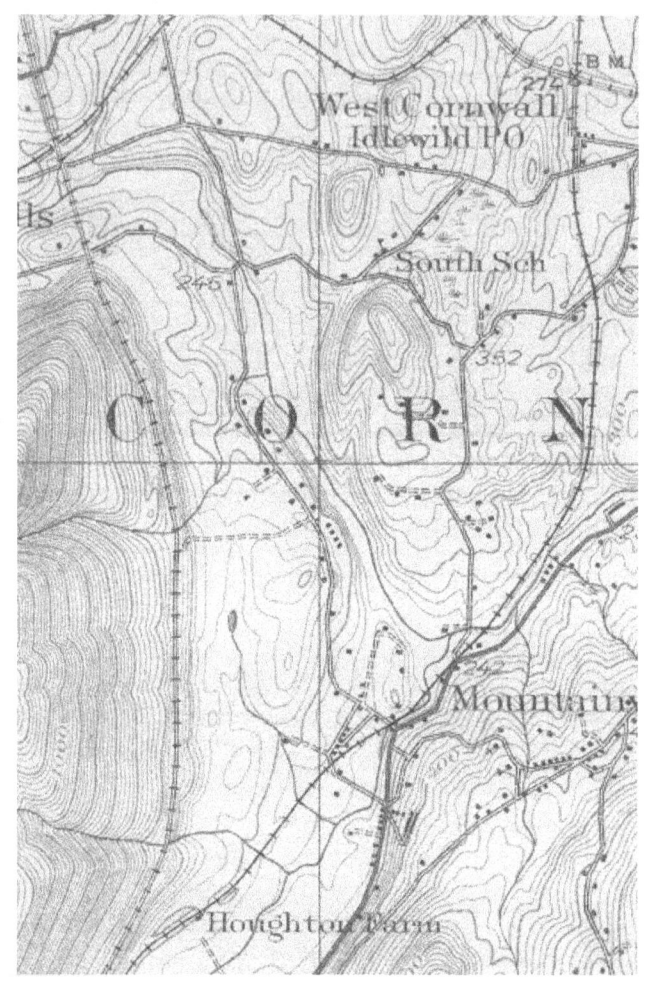

Houghton farm, in the last quarter of the 1800's, was a Model farm turned local landmark. An on site agricultural expert on farming gave lectures and performed experiments on every aspect of farm management. The noted artist, Winslow Homer, made a series of watercolors on farm life here. Inspired by the beauty of Houghton farm and the famous hospitality of its owners, the Valentine family.*
*Cornwall, New York, Images from the past 1988

(Above) Mountainville station (Standing, 2009) **(Below)** Ketcham's store was a Mountainville fixture for many years. When the station was still a Library I was there one afternoon when the Librarian asked me to watch the Library while she went to the post office. A small town feeling we are very much lacking in these parts these days.

(Next two pages) Woodbury station site
There were once two railroad bridges here, with the tracks of the short cut passing over its own bridge over Woodbury Creek before passing between the uprights of the Graham line trestle above. The station stood where the realigned highway (Rt. 32) passes through today. *Woodbury Historical society*

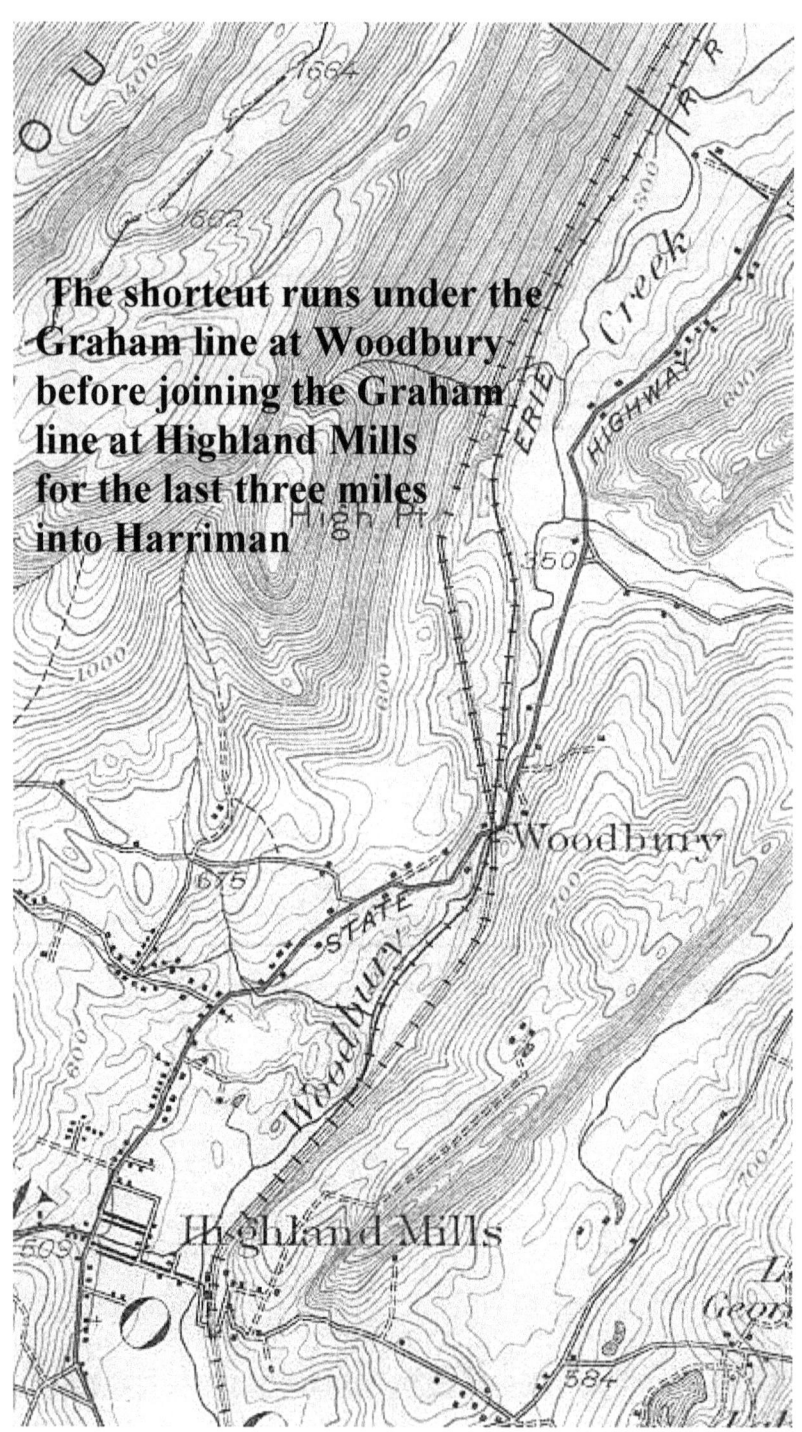

The shortcut runs under the Graham line at Woodbury before joining the Graham line at Highland Mills for the last three miles into Harriman

(Top) The "Tuxedo express" stopping at Highland Mills
The caption on the original picture reads: 'The Parlor car Porter hurries forward (left) with his "step" in hand".

(Bottom) Central Valley still stands, but altered and as private property
Both pictures, Woodbury Historical Society

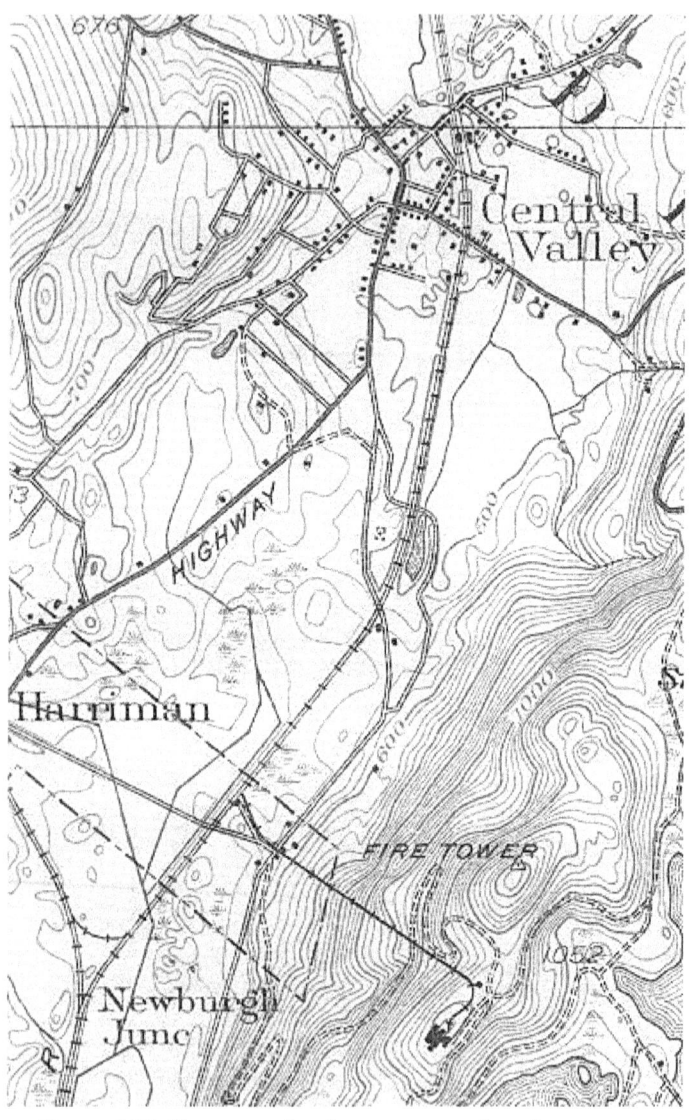

Central Valley was the last stop on the short cut before Harriman. At Harriman the triangle of the two Newburgh branches with the mainline is complete.

The first photo **(Below)** is of New York & Erie engine 109 at what is probably the first station in Newburgh, July 23, 1864.

The caption say's the fireman in the gangway with the black beard is William Kennedy. The second photo (Next page) was given to me by my grandmother. It was taken at Harriman, NY about 1905 or earlier. The man on the right is my grandfather, Fred Carpenter.

According to my grandmother he was firing the way freight from Newburgh for Engineer William Kennedy.

Forty years has put some gray in the beard, but I believe it is the same gentleman. *Dennis Carpenter*

(Below) The wye at Harriman, with the mainline leg left, the leg towards Central Valley on the right Ahead is looking towards Harriman with the Graham line behind us   (1991)

(Below) Postcard *Walter Kierzkowski*
Harriman station, just up from the wye where
the short cut/Graham line joined the Erie mainline

Recently demolished

One station on the mainline, which is still standing but not pictured here, is the station at Oxford Depot. Today it is a private property on the Oxford grade between Greycourt and Monroe.

(Next page) Monument that stood
by the Harriman station commemorating the first use
of the telegraph to issue train orders

Orders that were given by Erie Superintendent
Charles Minot to the Operator at Goshen to "Hold
for further orders to Conductor and Engineer day
express run to Goshen regardless of opposing train"

GOD WROUGHT

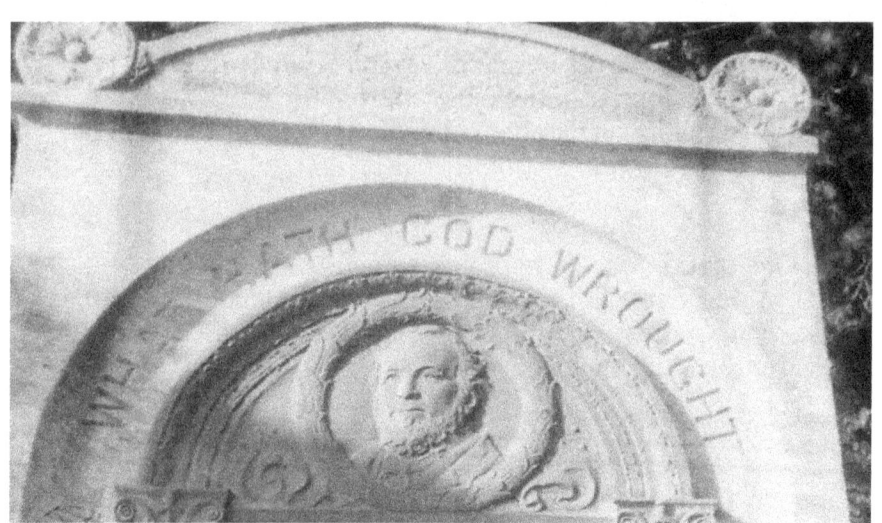

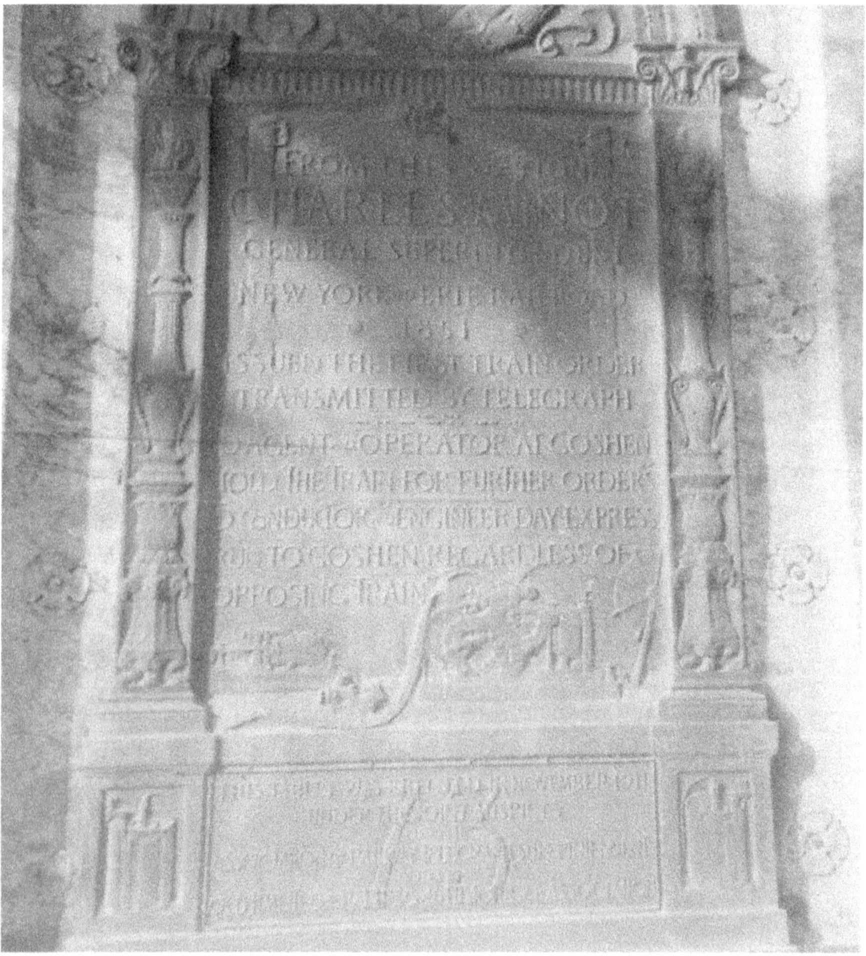
ISSUED THE FIRST TRAIN ORDER
TRANSMITTED BY TELEGRAPH
OPERATOR AT GOSHEN
HOLD THE TRAIN FOR FURTHER ORDERS

(Below) The Monroe station pictured here still stands, but altered and long since out of the railroad business. A later Monroe station, which stood a couple of hundred yards away, has since been lost to a fire.
Walter Kierzkowski

Chester station, beautifully restored as a museum
Volunteers Fred Kronk and Larry Neeb pose outside the station.

Outside of the triangle of the two Newburgh branches

Goshen station, renovated
Note the track signal, to the left, still in place

cupola, Goshen station

(Above) Newburgh's West Shore (New York Central) station (Under renovation)   The Erie's station stood across the tracks and to the right.
(Below) Port Jervis, another beautifully done renovation

The Newburgh branch

Craigville was the first stop on the
Newburgh branch after Greycourt.
No longer standing
Chester Historical Society

Enderlin, Washingtonville, and Craigville,
were replacement stations for earlier stations
stations lost to a fire*.

Railroadians of America 1991

**And Cornwall, N.Y. Images from the past* 1988
Friends of the Cornwall Public library*

(Top) 1967 *Dennis Carpenter* **(Bottom)** *Russell Hallock*
Salisbury Mills station was the last stop
before Vails Gate.
No longer standing

Dennis Carpenter was generous enough to not only send along his pictures, but also notes on this book and the branch. Put together they give a perspective of the branch that only a railroader or family of a railroader could know.

Page 53. Line was not double tracked that far. Erie probably made the O&W put it in "just in case they decided to put in another track. Double track was from Vails Gate Jct. to Newburgh with the second track continuing to just before RT.94 as a siding. At the end of this siding at Vails Gate Station is where the light engine turned over.

Page 63. Map: "STOCK HOUSE" next to station was known as the "RAG HOUSE" to Erie crews. "COAL SHED" track remained in service until the paper mill closed. Although by then it was a trestle and the shed had disappeared. Last car I saw on it was a N.Y.C. 55-ton hopper.

Page 67. Phone Box with Dispatcher phone was outside of Station until it burned.

Page 91. Switch curving to left was a team track that crossed the road to another Creamery. It was last used to unload Tank cars of fuel oil for Butefish Oil Co. They had storage tanks next to the old creamery.

Page 92. "Slate Cut" railroad location before Rt. 94 bridge

Page 96. "Clarks Cut" at top of hill. Two sisters of an Erie engineer lived there and would knit scarves and such for engine crews on the Branch.

Page 102. East leg of wye was removed after the end of steam. Branch main which was the west leg of the wye continued up and joined the Westbound Main under the L.&H.R. bridge. The north bridge carried the "MUD TRACK' which was a 11 car passing siding on the branch which ran out along the branch toward Craigville.

Page 105. Switch from the Newburgh Branch first joined a 70 car siding know as the "LONG" then joined the Westbound Main track up under the L.&H.R. bridge

Page 131. Switch to right went behind station and crossed Union Ave. to a coal company

Page 134. Houghton Farm was a Flag Stop at one time. When my Grandfather was engineer on the passenger motor cars, a farm employee lived in the station and would hand up bags of fruit and vegetables with a stick to the crew.

Page 150. Clove Road crossing. The passing track (south) in front of the station would be filled with Box cars for the Clark-Frost paper mill. This required much switching by the "Newburgh Night Haul". Maintence of Way Foreman Clark's daughter had a general store at the crossing. Good place to get ice cream while switching on a hot summer night or a cup of coffee in winter. She stayed open till the "Haul" went through.

We now leave the Newburgh branch and return to the O&W.

New York, Ontario & Western Railroad

Firthcliffe station   No longer standing

Firthcliffe was the only one out of all the O&W's two story, wood frame, stations between Cornwall and Middletown to receive the additional features of a spire, and Queen Anne style windows. Why exactly is still unclear, although an author's guess can be given here. The original owners of the textile mill across the street, which would within a few years become the Firth Carpet Company, wanted a station to impress. In the golden years when everything revolved around the local train station. The frame of one of these windows still survives, in this author's collection. The original station name of "Montana" was carved into the side of the station, below the peak, to the right.(Inset)

Next three pages: Orrs Mills station and trestle

Within a span of two miles the O&W Railway, once past Meadowbrook station and the Erie's two Newburgh branches, came through a nearly 90 degree curve before passing over its own towering trestle above Moodna creek. The trestle was sister in design to the Erie's landmark Moodna Viaduct. But At 110 feet high and 1,200 feet long, the O&W's trestle was only a third of the length and 83 feet shorter in height that her more famous sister five miles away. In the first half of the Twentieth century this trestle saw trains full of summer vacationers heading for the legendary Catskill resort region as well as coal trains coming from the Pennsylvania coal fields. Orrs Mills station stood just yards from the end of the trestle to the right in this picture. Firthcliffe station was about a mile to the left. Today only the trestle's massive abutments remain to tell the tale. **(Below)** Washer off the Orrs Mills trestle

Trestle pictures: *Ronald Vassallo*   NYOWRHS

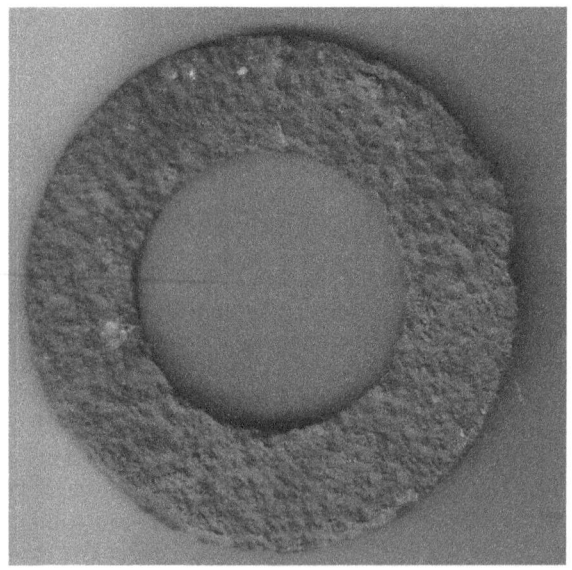

Orrs Mills trestle, looking from the Orrs Mills side

(Above) Taken on February, 23, 1946, at the time when the second track was out of service prior to removal **(Below)** 1964, about a year prior to it's dismantling. *Walter Kierzkowski* Moodna Creek was once called "Murderers' Creek" because of a family of settlers, according to local lore, who met their tragic fate at the hands of Indians. Moodna evolved from the Dutch word "Moordenaars" or "Murderers"

(Below) A remnant of when it was coal, not oil, that was keeping America moving
This machinery lay abandoned for many years in the old coal bin by the O&W's roadbed in Firthcliffe. Orrs Mills was also an important local coal supplier served by the O&W.

A vestige of simpler times: This small bridge on Orrs Mills Road near Enderlin is being replaced with a new, but featureless, concrete structure even as I write this in the summer of 2008. That arch behind the more "modern" concrete construction was the original one lane bridge.
Irene Sheldon

Middletown

Middletown has had no less than four railroad stations in it's history. One is a modern commuter shelter. The Middletown and New Jersey's Main street station is still in the railroad business. The Erie's station has taken on a new life as a Library. The O&W's massive station is still standing, but its future is in doubt.

The O&W's station clock was a familiar landmark to both Middletown residents and railroad passengers alike.

View from inside   *Ronald Vassallo*   NYOWRHS

South portal, O&W's Highview tunnel

Before leaving the O&W, the following pages contain a story that bears retelling.

The view from High View tunnel
Ron Britzke

THE New York, Ontario & Western Railway was mortally ill in the summer of 1954 when I went to work with the High View track gang. The "Old & Weary" had less than three years of its poverty-stricken history remaining. The handwriting was on the wall near the door

I spent a grueling but happy six months in that golden summer and lingering autumn, wielding a shovel with a handful of dedicated veterans as we tried to keep the deteriorating track in a semblance of operating shape for the few freights that rattled past.

They talked often about the railroad's increasingly bleak future. Would the Government step in and save the O&W? Could fresh business or capital be found? "They'll never let it die," they assured each other. As their world crumbled around them, they looked the other way and worked harder.

Something of the love those longtime employees felt for the rickety railroad rubbed off on me, and I shared their disappointment heartbreak for many when the rusty old line went under in 1957.

Life was bittersweet in 1954. I had a freshly minted college degree, but the looming military draft made the future uncertain. I needed temporary employment and found it at O&W headquarters in Middletown, N.Y. A summer track laborer was needed at High View on the Orange-Sullivan county border in southeastern New York near my home.

I reported to the section shanty on a bright, hot June Monday, meeting a reserved - even dubious - reception from Jim, the grizzled veteran foreman, and Bill, one of two laborers on regular duty. The other hand, Jerry, was ill that day. Jim and Bill both had been with the O&W about four decades, and the railroad was the central force of their lives. Jerry was younger and had been on the gang 10 years.

Jim, Bill, and I wheeled out our ancient motorcar in a ritual that was to become familiar as the weeks passed. Jim would start the engine with a crank - an uncertain procedure, particularly in cooler weather. I never looked underneath at the power plant, but it obviously had few cylinders (perhaps only one) and fired at about every other milepost. The exhaust was deafening; and at every tenth revolution, a shattering backfire disturbed the tranquility of the weed-cloaked right of way. Once this temperamental conveyance had warmed up, to the accompaniment of much fiddling with choke and throttle, we boarded and were off after Jim had called the dispatcher to get the whereabouts of the morning south- bound freight. "Past the Manor at 5:23," he'd announce gravely to us. This meant the train had gone through Livingston Manor on schedule and we had time to run from High View down to Winterton, the southern end of our section.

At Winterton, we took to an unused siding next to a boarded-up creamery - symbol of a vanished source of O&W business.

Eventually, the train would appear, usually with two or three F3 units trailed by too few revenue cars. With the main clear, we'd proceed to the site of that day's work. It was mostly the same - raising joints. Since the O&W was not ballasted on our section (or on most others), the procedure was simple. Bill inserted our big jack under a rail - one of several tasks he guarded with a jealous passion - and raised the track, exposing cavities under 10 or 12 ties on each side of the joint. The foreman knelt about 50 yards up the right of way and sighted down the rail, gesturing until the jack was high enough. We filled in under each raised tie with cinders from trackside, tamping the fresh material with a downward stroke of foot on shovel. Then it was on to the next joint to repeat the task.

One day, as I watched a train approach and a line of empty Buffalo Creek flour box cars dancing like drunken sailors over a section we'd just raised, I remarked cynically to Jerry that I saw no visible improvement from our labor. He just grinned and I got a sour look from Bill. We went on raising joints and the trains stayed on the crooked, wavering rails, so maybe we were doing something productive after all.

It was sweaty, dirty work. The cinders raised clouds of sooty dust. The right of way was carpeted with a deep blanket of the black stuff - a legacy from countless passages of Consolidations, Ten-Wheelers, Camelbacks, and other steamers which preceded the O&W's small fleet of diesels.

The High View station's guarded & sunken, rusting, sidetrack was all but hidden in weeds. I was surprised one morning to see a gondola parked there, I hadn't even been sure the switch worked. I peered over the side at a half load of new ties, fragrant with creosote. It took Jim hours of amortizing just to decide which of the crumbling ties on our section needed replacing most. We could have used up the whole allotment within sight of our shanty. This led to my only attempt at spiking. Bill was adept at it, smashing the spikes home with a few well-directed blows. Jerry wasn't bad either. I did most of the tie-shifting with, a huge pair of tongs while they hammered.

One day I demanded to try it. Jim handed me our oldest hammer, worn with years of use and probably twice as old as I was.

My first blow across the rail (I shunned the more cautious same-side approach) was a direct hit. I smirked as they giggled. The second shot hit the rail. The hammer head and half of the handle whizzed away into the woods like a scared pheasant, and my spiking career was spiked.

IN RETROSPECT, those days may not have been as enjoyable as they now seem through the mist of more than 20 years. But I can summon pleasant memories in abundance today . . . long-spanned gliders from the airport at Wurtsboro wheeling silently above us in the cloudless sky; the riotous racket of mating chipmunks racing through the dry leaves; the sun's first glow piercing the ground mist on a damp September morning.

And things were seldom dull on the O&W. There came a day when Jim, who was somewhat hard of hearing, knelt to resight a joint after we had raised it and removed the jack. A freight rounded the curve behind him. We called a warning. Engrossed in his calculations, he missed it.

We waved with increasing vigor. He finally looked back. By this time, the train was fairly close. He retreated in haste and jerked his arm up and down twice as the engine passed a signal for the engineer to blow the air horn next time.

The crew grinned down at us, but I gave the hogger a middle-finger salute, thinking that he damn well should have hit the horn as a courtesy to an aging man whose knees had long since lost youth's agility.

I was laid off briefly in August, collecting a graduation present from my parents a - British-built Triumph motorcycle. That transformed the 8-mile trip to and from work. I swooped joyously over the undulating back roads between home and High View, lunchbox slung over my shoulder with a rope. I parked my shiny new beast in an empty shack which still stands at the mouth of the tunnel.

The tunnel was also Jim's rainy-day work backup. We occasionally sharpened tools in the shanty during storms, but most of our implements were worn beyond a fine hone anyway.

We cleared rock from the tunnel ditches when it rained. The bore was only partially lined, and the brittle slate of the roof crumbled with monotonous regularity.

The yearly rockfall was substantial enough to require attention from the Scranton "extra gang" every winter. I met this crew once, when we changed a rail early in my stay. Most of the extras were young, and of Polish or Slavic extraction, I judged. They did their work with insolent expertise, drank Finkle's Tavern dry of beer during their overnight stay at Summitville, then moved on.

On the weekend before Thanksgiving, I was laid off for good and said farewell to my companions.

Jerry and I had developed a warm friendship, and the taciturn reserve of Jim and Bill had thawed Occasionally. Now it was over.

I was 3000 miles away in 'Los Angeles, savoring trips to the Tehachapi Loop and working in the motorcycle industry when the O&W went under. But even before that, the High View gang had broken up.

Jerry quit soon after I left and went on to other things. Mercifully, Jim did not see the end of his life's work. He retired and died quietly six months later as the O&W swayed on the brink of oblivion.

Bill - fierce, square-jawed, touchy - stayed to the finish. Forty years a track laborer, he was proud, of his many skills as only a man of little education and limited horizons could be. When the O&W died Bill's light went out.

A year or two later, firemen were called to High View one night and found the section shanty aflame. They put out the blaze and discovered Bill's body in the ashes.

WHAT did it all mean? I stand at the gaunt, silent tunnel portal today and find no answer. More than 20 years have fled since I drove away from High View on that last icy November afternoon, and the past is as irretrievable as the future is unknown. The weeds finally won and the forgotten right of way is vanishing.

My thoughts are far away as a distant rumble intrudes. The morning southbound at the far portal? A change in engine pitch breaks the spell as a twin-stacked International Transtar heads down old Route 17 with a load that might have gone l.c.l. if the Old & Weary had survived. There is a small ache in my throat as I straddle the motorcycle which brought me to High View once more. A throb of power beckons me back to today, and the shadows of another time fade in the shimmer of heat waves along the highway.

Trains Magazine 1975

Abridged version of original larger article

© 2009 TRAINS Magazine. Reprinted with permission of Kalmbach Publishing Co. All rights reserved

Twilight on the Newburgh branches
Erie Petition-1920's
From the pages of the Cornwall Local

As the 1920's dawned there were two mindsets in America: A new generation that had fallen in love with the Automobile was bringing to an end the American Railroad's glory days as the prime mover of the country's goods and passengers. In this new economy the railroads as a business found themselves having to take a hard look as to what stations were no longer profitable. But at the same time the railroad station was still for many too important a part of the daily life they had known to let go.

In 1921 The Erie railroad filed a petition with the New York Public service commission, case number 158, to discontinue the employment of station agents at Grand view, Gulf summit, Oxford, Woodbury, Enderlin, Craigville and New Windsor.

Hearings were held that August at Middletown and Newburgh to a courtroom of attorneys and town Supervisors representing their districts and the patrons of the stations who were opposed to the Erie's petition.

A full public hearing was to be held In New York on September 15th, at a session of the Public Service Commission. On the 2nd of September a petition had already been filed by the Erie, removing Woodbury station from the original petition.

The outcome of the hearing on the 15th denied the removal of Agents at Oxford, Enderlin, Grand View and Gulf Summit out of public necessity.

Full time Agents at Craigville and New Windsor could be discontinued under the following conditions that would not inconvenience the public:

Attendants shall still be employed whose duties are to keep the station and grounds clean, orderly, and when necessary, properly lighted and heated.

The buildings must be opened fifteen minutes prior to scheduled arrival of trains and until after the departure of trains. Specifically mentioned in the order was in the case of New Windsor and Craigville was the daily trains 361, 354, and 367.

Provisions also had to be made to ensure that all incoming and outgoing freight shipments were properly received or safely locked away until picked up by their rightful owners.

As the next three decades wore on, the number of petitions the railroads filed to close unprofitable stations and whole rail lines were to only increase, while the number of voices against the closing would only shrink. In 1921 the handwriting was already on the wall.

Snake Hill, New Windsor   1971
Dennis Carpenter

(Below and next page) E-L engine 1239   1970's
Russell Hallock

(Above) Blooming Grove, 1971 Sheffield's Creamery building in the background *Dennis Carpenter*

(Left) Highland Mills tower in the distance beyond station

Highland Mills, (station site to the left, in the brush) where the tracks of the short cut joined the Graham line for the last three miles into Harriman.

The Graham line is to the right. And to the left, this last surviving piece of trackage at the junction fades into the mist and into history. *Inset picture, Woodbury Historical Society*

We will finish our walk along the Erie with a look at one of the most picturesque areas of the Newburgh branch.

Photo Gallery: Under the shadow of Schunemunk* Mountain Salisbury Mills/ Mountainville N.Y.

* 1902 spelling USGS

(Top) Orrs Mills Road
(Bottom) Clove Road, with Otterkill Road in the distance **(Next two)** Otterkill Road

Views from top of Moodna Viaduct
(Below) Looking over Orrs Mills Road

Schunemunk from Otterkill Road

(Top) Otterkill road   **(Bottom)** Clove Road

(Top) Clove Road **(Bottom)** Station Road

Woodcock Road **(Next two pages)** Coming into Mountainville

(Top) Pleasant Hill Road   The Thruway in the distance crosses the former Erie roadbed.   **(Bottom)** Taylor Road

(Bottom) We are at Woodbury Creek, looking from the site of one of several bridges the Erie crossed coming into Mountainville. The top picture was taken from the abutment shown below.

Two roads diverged in a yellow wood,
And sorry I could not travel both
And be one traveler, long I stood
And looked down one as far as I could
To where it bent in the undergrowth;

Then took the other, as just as fair,
And having perhaps the better claim,
Because it was grassy and wanted wear;
Though as for that the passing there
Had worn them really about the same,

And both that morning equally lay
In leaves no step had trodden black.
Oh, I kept the first for another day!
Yet knowing how way leads on to way,
I doubted if I should ever come back.

I shall be telling this with a sigh
Somewhere ages and ages hence:
Two roads diverged in a wood, and I—
I took the one less traveled by,
And that has made all the difference.

    Robert Frost

Milk bottle from Sweet Clover Farms Mountainville, N.Y.
Author's collection

www.ingramcontent.com/pod-product-compliance
Lightning Source LLC
Chambersburg PA
CBHW032043150426
43194CB00006B/409